LISTEN TO ME!

The voices of pupils with emotional and behavioural difficulties (EBD)

Susan Wise

Published by Lucky Duck Publishing Ltd.,
3 Thorndale Mews, Bristol BS8 2HX

Illustrations by Philippa Drakeford
Cover design by Barbara Maines
Book design by Helen Weller
Reprinted February 2002
Printed in the UK by The Book Factory, Mildway Avenue, London N1 4RS

Foreword

This book is dedicated to Pat.

I would like to thank Christi for encouraging me throughout the writing of this book, Graham Upton for his support and advice in completing the research and finally the pupils who gave me their time and thoughts.

Contents

Introduction

This book offers its readers the opportunity to listen to pupils described as having emotional and behavioural difficulties (EBD). It offers fascinating insight into their behaviour and the various aspects of themselves and their lives that they consider to have influenced that behaviour. Their honest and thought provoking perspectives are presented throughout the book providing any teacher or professional who works with such pupils a unique opportunity to *simply listen*. As a classroom teacher myself for over fifteen years in both mainstream and special education, I believe that this is something that educators should seek to do. I believe that listening to those children whose behaviour disturbs us is an essential step towards understanding them and meeting their needs. However, I recognise that given the time involved in completing ever-increasing day to day workloads and meeting the exhausting practical demands of classroom life, it isn't always realistic. In order to help busy professionals gain the valuable insights into what their pupils would like to tell them about their difficulties, I completed a research study for my Ph.D. (Wise, 1997) that focused on recording and analysing the thoughts of some children who had struggled in mainstream schools. Believing that the results of my research were of value to a wide audience I have written this book for anyone who wants to hear the perspectives of children with EBD and who believes these children have something worth saying. Throughout the book I have provided summaries of important points and have encouraged readers to reflect on their current practices and to consider possible changes to their own schools or classrooms that may result in their improved success with children with EBD.

In chapters 1 and 2 I offer some brief background to the study and to the pupils who were interviewed. In chapters 3 and 4 I present exactly what the pupils said about the factors and processes that had influenced their behaviour and also the meanings and motives behind these behaviours. For those readers interested in a little more academic detail I have included an appendix and also refer to my original thesis.

Finally, I have of course changed the names of the pupils and their schools but do wish to thank them for their wonderful contribution to this publication!

1 Trying to understand children with EBD

Before I attempted to probe into and hopefully reveal the hidden worlds of my pupils' minds there were some issues that I felt were essential to consider.

- Why do we want to better understand those children who do not conform or who challenge authority?

- What exactly do we mean by EBD and what theories help us to understand related behaviours?

- How can we increase our understanding of the behaviour of children with EBD?

- What are the nature, extent and impact of previous and current attempts at exploring the perceptions of children with EBD?

Some possible answers to these questions are briefly outlined.

Why do we want to better understand those children who do not conform or who challenge authority?

The answer to this question may at first appear obvious but it forces us to explore the possible motives behind any attempts to better understand the behaviour of pupils with EBD and to clarify the use to which such enquiry should be put and its true value.

At the highest level of policy making and funding, money is inevitably an important consideration for those dealing with the disturbing and rapidly increasing number of pupils who are being excluded permanently from mainstream schools and who need alternative provision, (Parsons & Howlett, 1996, Times Educational Supplement, 1996a,b). Excluded pupils and school refusers create a significant financial responsibility for any educational budget and it has been stated that educating a child outside the mainstream school can be four or five times more expensive than providing education within the

Financial Considerations

Educating children outside mainstream schools is expensive.

9

mainstream setting (Parsons, 1996, Daily Telegraph, 1996). Clearly research that may lead to the maintenance of more pupils within the mainstream setting, and reduce the need for 'special' facilities could be considered important for economic reasons regardless of the needs of the individual.

The Need for Control

An improved understanding of deviant behaviour may be used to maintain social control which can be perceived as a lack of appreciation or acceptance of individuality

Maintaining or enforcing control may be another somewhat controversial motive for governmental or societal interest in research into the behaviour of deviants, including pupils with EBD. Depending on personal opinion, striving for such control may be considered a positive or negative goal. Deviancy in any society is a threat to social calm, and social calm is usually considered important in the functioning of a society including its schools. However, Meighan (1986) cites Berger as describing the sociologist who carries out research as a spy, and questions the potential use of sociological findings, suggesting that the findings of sociological inquiry may be used by anyone 'whose activities involve the manipulation of people...' (p8). Clearly, an elimination of social deviancy is in the interest of those invested in a smooth running society or school. But it may also reflect an intolerance for expressions of 'individuality', (Schostak, 1983), and an unquestioning attitude to the norms and values of that environment. This approach suggests that the environment itself is without need of change and that all individuals within it must adapt their behaviour to meet its expectations or be removed to a more controlled environment. Whatever you believe regarding the control of people in our society and schools it is important to recognise that research into the behaviour of difficult children may be motivated by more than a desire to better support and meet their needs.

Improving Provision

A better understanding of behaviour may lead to more appropriate and successful provision for challenging children.

A third reason for research, and that which motivated me to undertake the study presented in this book, is a concern with helping to ensure that those pupils who struggle within our current education system are given the best possible opportunity to succeed and fulfil the potential they have. Such research may simply aim to gain a better understanding of why pupils behave in certain ways in the hope of bringing about changes in the child's environment that may facilitate improved success and happiness in their lives. Such research should assist professionals in their consideration of what actually is 'best' for those pupils whose behaviour deviates from the norm. To achieve this, decisions need to be made regarding where the focus of change should be and these decisions are closely linked to the various theories of behaviour that have been proposed over the years. Current theories involve varying degrees of focus either on the individual, or on the systems surrounding the individual and they lead on to our second important question for consideration.

What exactly do we mean by EBD and what theories help us to understand it?

Describing Behaviour

Finding appropriate terminology to describe and categorise behaviour is difficult.

Categorising and defining behaviour can be a dangerously subjective task. Behaviour is always open to interpretation, and often it cannot be interpreted without consideration of its context. For many years those working in the education field have struggled with attempts to firstly find an appropriate all encompassing term for the behaviours being displayed by disturbing pupils, and secondly to better understand the nature of these behaviours using various theories and models of behaviour. It is important for the reader to consider these issues and to take the opportunity to consider their own beliefs regarding theoretical aspects of behaviour. One's theoretical preference may powerfully influence the terminology chosen to describe disturbing children and Cooper (1996) believes that it is necessary and valuable to become aware of potential problems that can arise as a result of labelling pupils based on their behaviour.

Theoretical beliefs influence how we label behaviour and this can in turn impact that behaviour

For some years the various theories of behaviour were consistently placed in clearly separate or discrete categories and these theories are comprehensively described in numerous publications (Charlton & David, 1993, Cooper, Smith & Upton, 1994). For the purpose of this study I adopted theories of behaviour loosely termed interactionist. Such theories accept that people are able to interpret their own behaviour and make decisions based on their perceptions of situations. These theories reject the somewhat more traditional psychodynamic or social learning theories of behaviour which suggest that behaviour is a result of subconscious forces or drives working to control the individual. In the case of psychodynamic theories these forces, considered to have resulted from earlier experiences particularly during childhood, work from inside to control the individual. Social learning theory focuses more on the powerful forces within society that control an individual's behaviour, again offering little opportunity for the individual to make conscious decisions.

Theories of Behaviour

There are a number of different theories of behaviour, including psychodynamic, social learning and interactionism.

Interactionism accepts that individuals interpret experiences and make decisions about their behaviour.

Interactionism has been developed in various ways, and currently presents itself in the shape of systemic or ecological approaches to behaviour. These approaches are concerned with the context of a behaviour, or the systems in which the individual lives, and in particular the way in which these systems interact with that individual and thus influence his or her behaviour. (Apter, 1982, Upton & Cooper, 1990). Such approaches emphasise the importance of the pupil's environment to his or her behaviour, without focusing solely on the individual. The systemic approach does not focus solely on the behaviour of a pupil as being a result of an inner problem or conflict or as being a product of social learning. Instead it encourages a belief that problems can potentially lie within the systems surrounding the pupil, or at least in the interaction between the child and these systems. Clearly a systemic approach offers increased opportunities for intervention including not only the child but also the environment itself and the attitudes of individuals who are involved with the child.

Current Theories

Systemic or ecological theories of behaviour encourage the consideration of behaviour in context.

Such theories provide increased opportunity for intervention or support by considering the environment and how it interacts with the child.

So there are a number of different theories of behaviour and an understanding of these different theories when working with pupils with EBD is essential in deciding upon educational strategies and interventions. There is also a developing theoretical view that confining oneself to a rigid belief in just one theory when interpreting or defining disturbing behaviour is dangerously limiting. Cooper (1999) believes that given the diversity of the problems experienced by pupils with EBD a similar diversity of approaches is needed. There certainly seems to be a danger in polarising and oversimplifying the theoretical starting points from which behaviour can be investigated. Apter (1982) encourages the acknowledgement of both the internal (psychological) and external (sociological) driving forces on a person, and proposes an ecological theory for behaviour. He states; ' ...it is the interaction between them which always accounts for behaviour.' (p16).

Using an Eclectic Approach

The problems experienced by EBD children are diverse, therefore the approaches and interventions used to support them must not be based on polarised or oversimplified theoretical starting points.

Using Pupils' Perceptions

Factors or forces that drive behaviour may be conscious, subconscious, external or internal.

Pupils' perceptions of the factors and processes that have influenced their behaviour should be explored.

This book is based on the belief that there is a need to acknowledge that important contributions may be made by any of the various sociological and psychodynamic theories in analysing and understanding the behaviour of pupils with EBD. I believe that there is probably a highly complex interaction of conscious, unconscious, internal and external driving forces on each individual that contributes to their behaviours. For pupils with EBD it is important that we explore all the factors and processes that are perceived by these pupils as significant in relation to their behaviour and subsequent placement in a special needs setting. With my research I attempted to do just that and my results are presented in this book. I have also attempted to offer an enhanced understanding of exactly why or how different factors and processes interact and become significant in impacting behaviour and based on this information have made proposals for improving educational provision and experiences for pupils with EBD.

How can we increase our understanding of the behaviour of children with EBD?

Seeking Causes or Reasons for Behaviour

A positivist approach to behaviour explores the causes for behaviour, seeking patterns between social variables and behaviour.

Finding reasons for behaviour involves questioning individuals in order to gain their interpretation of their actions.

Soon after starting my project I realised that studying behaviour is certainly a complex task! Scherer, Gersch & Fry (1990) describe human behaviour as having '…infinite variability and complexity…' (pxiv) and explain how behaviour can remain totally unpredictable even when artificial situations are created and attempts are made to reduce options under experimental conditions. Still we remain dedicated to seeking patterns and being able to predict and understand behaviour. Certainly there are some aspects of a person's social background and environment, and also some psychological variables that make predictions concerning behaviour quite feasible and much research has vigorously sought out such factors. Such research has utilised many different methodological techniques with the choice of such techniques resting to some extent with the specific aims of the research. For example Wolff (1993) stresses that there is a difference in seeking reasons for behaviour as opposed to causes. Theories that propose direct causal explanations for behaviour, defined traditionally as positivist, (Woods, 1977), assume that universal laws determine social behaviour, that social facts are observable and measurable, and that research can reveal relationships between these facts and certain behaviours. These relationships allow causal statements about behaviour to be made, and future behaviour may be predicted using such patterns. Of course such theory removes any responsibility for behaviour from the control of the individual. Reasons for behaviour may however be considered as quite different to causes. Those who explore reasons believe that the individual carries out a degree of interpretation prior to their actions. Thus, there are no predictable patterns of behaviour because each individual makes sense of his or her world and acts according to his or her own feelings and the meanings that they attribute to different situations. The individual in this case is therefore potentially able to account for his or her behaviour in terms of personal reasons or motives. The methodology utilised in seeking such data may be quite different to that used to simply correlate specific variables with certain behaviours.

Interviewing as a Research Technique

For the purpose of my study I adopted a methodological approach that enabled the pupils with EBD to tell me the reasons for their behaviour. As my focus was on gaining insight into all the various factors that may have influenced their behaviour I chose the common ethnographic methodology, interviewing. For many researchers in this field interviewing has provided the most suitable opportunity for pupils to share their perceptions and based on the success of previous studies using this technique, I considered it to be the most appropriate for my needs.

There are however a number of criticisms of interviewing as a technique for seeking the hidden thoughts of individuals. One concern is the extent to which there exists an objective reality that can be found through an interview. The true value of an individual's own unique reality has created much debate amongst those involved in researching deviant behaviour, particularly through qualitative methodologies. In particular, some have doubted the value of perspectives gained from children, and in particular children displaying difficult or disturbing behaviours, whose perspectives they consider to have been altered by their emotional states. As Lubbe (1986) states; '...I have sought to show how powerfully pupils' emotional states and conflicts constrict their perception of, and subsequent dealings with, teachers - and psychotherapists.' (p34). He describes certain 'disturbed' children's views on teachers as 'misperceptions' (p35), which suggests they are distorted in some way and therefore hold no real value.

Seeking the 'reality' of another in research is of course a somewhat complex task. Cooper et al (1994) state that to truly understand behaviour there is a need to accept subjectivity, '...different people place different interpretations on what happens around them, according to their view of the world, and thus *construct* their own views of reality.' (p16). Similarly, Woods (1983) states; 'Of course we shall never be able to get into another's mind to see exactly how it is working.' (p17). It appeared to me that the closest I could try to get into the minds of my pupils was to conduct informal interviews with them and to encourage their spontaneous and open responses to my questions. Cullingford (1991) states that 'What children say is the clearest and most revealing insight into their minds.' (p8).

What are the nature, extent and impact of previous and current attempts at exploring the perceptions of children with EBD?

Certainly the right of a child to be heard and the opportunity for a child to express thoughts and perceptions have grown over the years. 'Children should be seen and not heard' is a familiar statement from Victorian times which clearly reflects the extent to which society at that time placed little value on its children and what they were thinking. In fact if we explore deeper into our history, we find not only a desire that children should be denied a voice and have an almost total lack of rights, but also abuse and exploitation. Although sadly in many parts of the world such attitudes and actions remain, in the U.K. in recent years some serious steps have been taken both within the legislature and policies of social services and education to ensure children's rights. Such legal changes possibly reflect a major change in the way children are viewed in our society although the true value of young people and their thoughts and opinions and the amount of power we should allow them to hold remain controversial. The role they take in our society and the degree of

Interviewing is a commonly used technique in ethnographic research.

Pupils' Perceptions

Can pupils' perceptions be considered 'accurate'?

Exploring Another Person's Reality

We can never get inside another's mind but interviewing may be the closest we get.

The Rights of Children

Our attitude to children and their rights has changed since the 'seen and not heard' Victorian days.

Legal changes within social services and education reflect a willingness to recognise their value in our society, although this remains a controversial issue.

status that we attribute to them is still an area of confusion for parents and professionals alike.

Legal Obligations

We are now legally bound to explore pupils' perspectives during certain educational procedures.

The 1989 Children's Act entitled children in care to see their files, resulted in booklets for the children themselves stating their rights and instructed courts to consider the child's own personally stated needs. Advances have also been made to extend the educational rights of children, including the 1993 Education Act (DES, 1993), the Code of Practice (DES, 1994) and also certain OFSTED (Office for Standards in Education) documents. These and various other publications all contain statements that stress the importance of obtaining the pupils' perspective and there are now standard procedures that must involve pupils in their own education such as pupil profiling, records of achievement and special needs assessments. Publications that present these developments in some depth include Davie, Upton & Varma (1996) and Davie & Galloway (1996).

Moral Obligations

Children should be given the opportunity to articulate their views.

The perspectives of children may differ from those of other parties and should be utilised when seeking to develop good practice.

These developments may reflect a growing awareness not only of legal obligations to children, but also as Cooper (1993a) states a moral obligation '...to enable pupils to articulate their views as effectively as possible.' (p129). Cooper (1993a) states that the pupils' views '...provide us with a richly textured account that is available from no other source.' (p129), and Branwhite (1994) agrees; '...the opinions which teenage children give are based upon first-hand experiences and sources of personal information not wholly available to professionals,' (p66). This growing awareness and acceptance that children's perspectives may be very different to those of parents, teachers and other professionals allows the child to contribute to decisions regarding their behaviour and education. Cooper (1993a) states:

> '...the pupils' perspectives taken in conjunction with other evidence can help us to identify models of good practice that enable us to develop deep insights into the nature and treatment of EBD.' (p129).

The True Impact of the Pupil's Views

Despite offering an increasing voice to children, are we really giving weight to that voice or empowering the child?

Despite these positive statements concerning the importance of seeking and utilising pupil perspectives in certain situations, a debate continues as to the true impact of such pupil involvement. Garner (1993a) acknowledges growing attempts at obtaining pupil perspectives but expresses concern over the use to which they have been put. Regarding pupils who have been excluded or who have displayed disruptive behaviours he states that; 'There has been little evidence that the views of these students concerning their schooling have been used to develop or refine school procedures or professional practice.' (p102). If this is the case, then reasons for this lack of impact should be discussed. It may be that we wrongly assume that by giving children the opportunity to speak that we are empowering them. As Troyna (1994) points out, we should not be misled into believing that 'giving a voice' to suppressed or oppressed or disadvantaged groups is the same as empowering them. He stresses that empowerment does not follow automatically from giving a voice, as there may be significant differences between the two.

Additionally, there are those who question the ability of young people to articulate or actually reveal perceptions that hold any value, and this may limit the desire to gain or utilise their perceptions. Cullingford (1991) describes this as:

' ...an ancient sense of egotism in adults. We know so much more than children and can explain so much more precisely that children are, in contrast, limited. This leads to an unexamined assumption that children do not really know what they think...' (p6).

This may reflect the continued imbalance of power in our society between adults and children and the low status of the children's role. (See Calvert cited in Meighan, 1986 p34). Despite numerous examples of research where pupils have been very articulate in expressing their thoughts and opinions, their perceptions continue to be scrutinised in terms of their accuracy or objectivity. This inability or unwillingness to accept the perceptions or subjective reality of our pupils potentially impedes the effective involvement of young people in educational decision making. Galloway, Ball, Blomfield & Seyd (1982) believe that each professional has his or her own philosophy regarding the perceptions of disruptive pupils:

'The importance teachers, sociologists and psychologists attach to pupils' accounts of their own disruptive behaviour depends on their philosophy. At one end of the spectrum is the view that pupils cannot be sufficiently objective to give any valid or meaningful account of their own experiences at school.... at the other end of the spectrum is the view that only pupils' accounts of disruptive behaviour should be taken seriously.' (p47).

An example of this is revealed by Meighan cited in Galloway et al (1982), who sought the permission of some head teachers to allow pupils to offer opinions of lessons given by student teachers. Although most agreed, one or two refused, '...claiming among other things that the pupils lacked the objectivity and maturity to make such judgements...' (p47). Keys & Fernandes (1993), who carried out a major study into mainstream school pupils' perceptions of schooling, also appear to have some doubts by making the following statement:

'Most of the conclusions of this study have been based on students' perceptions of their schools and their teachers, which may not of course, always accurately reflect life in school.' (p I-63).

They follow this statement however with a positive comment regarding the importance of pupils' perceptions:

'However, it should be borne in mind that students' perceptions of school and teachers are of paramount importance and are likely to be a major influence on their behaviour in school and attitudes towards education.' (p I-63).

Further evidence for the reluctance or inability of the adult world to truly value the pupil perspective comes from Wade & Moore (1993) who found that in a survey of mainstream primary and secondary school teachers, less than a third said that they took account of the views of their pupils. They report that '...many regarded consultation with pupils to be time consuming, valueless and irrelevant, leading to the creation of problems and a wasting of time.' (p179). Clearly if mainstream pupils are still being ignored then there

The Status of Children

Some people still question the validity of children's perspectives considering pupils too immature to make sound judgements, and consultation with young people as wasting time and creating problems

Others state that a pupil's perceptions of his or her school and teachers are very important, influencing behaviour and attitudes.

The Needs of Others

Do we consider children as equal clients within the system or are the needs of adults more powerful?

is certainly a danger that the perceptions of pupils with EBD will be considered to be of even less value, owing to their 'disturbed' or 'emotional' state. Tisdall & Dawson (1994) state that this may be the case 'despite the child-focus claims by special education teachers.' (p179).

There may be a further reason as to why the child's perspective is often disregarded. Armstrong, Galloway & Tomlinson, (1993) describe how a child's contribution to the assessment procedure for special needs may be minimal, not because those professionals involved in the assessment are unaware of, or unwilling to take into account the child's perspective, but because there are adult clients (schools, parents, LEA's) who have more power to affect the outcome of the assessment. In other words '...it may not be 'poor practice' that leads to the child's perspective being disregarded but rather the demands of a complex situation in which the needs of the competing clients ... determine the extent to which the child's perspective is *allowed to be relevant*.' (p130). Harris (1994) has similar concerns about the apparent opportunities for pupils to share views and perceptions as part of their records of achievement. She considers that their true value is limited by the greater concerns of schools, such as accountability, productivity and efficiency. It would seem that even if we accept the subjective reality of our pupils as being of value and not false or distorted in someway, then we must also be prepared to consider them equally as clients within the system, along with the professionals, parents and schools. This equality is essential if we are to pay more than lip service to their opinions and perspectives, and do more than just listen to or record their views. I hope that this book will provide evidence to support and confirm the value of the perceptions of pupils.

Research

There is increasing research into the perspectives of pupils, but will results impact policy and practice?

Research that has sought pupils' perspectives has increased over recent years and is well documented, (Meighan, 1986, Kutnick & Jules, 1993, Cooper et al, 1994). Although there are some surprisingly early relevant publications dating back to the 1930's through to the 1960's, most research worthy of particular note is more recent, including Hargreaves (1967), Blishen (1969), Furlong (1977), Tattum (1982), Schostak (1983), Reid (1985), Cronk (1987), Woods (1980,1990), and Ruddock, Chaplain & Wallace (1995). This research tends to either use pupil perspectives alongside a range of other perspectives and data as part of a general enquiry into schooling issues, or concentrates solely on the pupils' views of one or more specific issues. Much has been focused on mainstream schooling and uses the perspectives of pupils within the mainstream setting, whereas fewer have been concerned with special needs pupils and their perspectives of schooling. Certain publications during the last decade do however reflect an increasing interest in researching the perceptions of special education pupils, (Lloyd-Smith & Davies, 1995, Davies, 1996). But special education is a broad term encompassing many varied needs and I believe that there remains inadequate interest or research focusing on the behaviour and needs of pupils with EBD and in particular research that seeks the perspectives of these pupils. An increasing concern over the number of pupils being excluded from mainstream schools has resulted in some valuable attempts at exploring the perceptions of such pupils. (Johns, 1996, Cullingford & Morrison, 1996, De Pear, 1997) yet it remains to be seen whether such publications will have any impact on policy and procedure.

I hope that this book will offer you an opportunity to better understand your pupils with EBD and increase your respect for these pupils' unique views and interpretations of their own behaviour. I have tried to offer you the reader a new focus concerning the perspectives of pupils with EBD by revealing the wide range of factors that the pupils themselves perceive as influencing their behaviour. By reading the reasons given by the pupils for their behaviour and my practical suggestions and tips based on these statements, I hope that you will be better able to understand your pupils' needs and offer them more appropriate and successful educational support and opportunity.

This Book

What influences pupils' behaviour and what can you do to support them and meet their needs?

2 The children, their schools and the interviews

In this chapter I give a very brief outline of the methodology used for my study. Any reader requiring more detail should refer to my original study (Wise, 1997).

The children and their schools

36 pupils (31 boys and 5 girls) were interviewed, aged 12 to 16 years old. They all attended one of two special educational establishments for pupils with EBD and represented a broad spectrum of challenging behaviours. I knew the children I interviewed as I was working in both of the schools at the time of interviewing.

The Oakwood Centre is part of the Home and Hospital Teaching Service (HHTS) for the area in which it is located. There are on average 25 to 30 girls and boys attending the Centre at any one time. The pupils are either psychiatric patients from a nearby adolescent psychiatric unit or young people from the local area whose needs cannot be met in the mainstream setting. Interview data was collected from a total of 16 pupils attending the Centre, 5 of whom were girls. All were white and from both middle and working class homes. None of those interviewed was at that time a patient at the psychiatric unit.

Southdown School is an EBD day school educating approximately 60 boys aged 7 to 16 years of age who are mostly white and from working class homes. 20 pupils attending the school were interviewed from a total of 35 boys on role in year groups 7 to 11. All pupils in these year groups were invited to participate and although none refused a number were not interviewed owing to being absent or unavailable at the time of interviewing.

Collecting and studying the children's contributions

I used an informant style of interview (Powney & Watts, 1987) which allowed the children the freedom to respond and give information as he or she saw fit. This contrasts to a respondent style of interview during which responses are made more rigidly to a fixed set of questions, pre-set by the interviewer. I had identified a number of broad areas of enquiry and a series of standard trigger questions associated with each of these areas in order to focus the children on certain relevant issues (see appendix). The broad areas of enquiry that I considered valuable were:

- The history and nature of the pupils' schooling difficulties.

- Aspects of school and schooling associated with the pupils' difficulties. (Including attitudes towards special needs provision).

- The significance of social, family or life events in the pupils' difficulties.

- The psychological or physiological aspects of the pupils' difficulties and their attitudes to treatment or professional support.

- The behaviour of the pupils in response to their difficulties.

No one interview was ever the same as another in terms of questioning, consistent with the total individuality of each pupil and their own individual experiences and responses. However, in each case the opening area of enquiry that I chose to investigate was that of early memories of school, a topic that most interviewees felt comfortable discussing. More difficult or sensitive issues were raised later when my relationship with the interviewee had developed and there was an increased degree of confidence and trust.

Interviewing at the Oakwood Centre took place over a period of one year and some pupils were interviewed more than once. At Southdown the pupils were interviewed just once throughout the course of one term. Each interview was of one half to one hour's duration and was taped. I discussed issues of confidentiality and each pupil was allowed to negotiate the time and place of interviews and was also free to stop an interview at any time.

Questions about the methodology

There are important comments and criticisms associated with highly qualitative research and the use of interviewing as a data collection technique. Some of the most significant points are listed here.

- **Should more than one technique be used to obtain data?**

Perhaps there is a need to utilise more than one technique in attempting to obtain insight into pupils' experiences. Some researchers have used pupils' responses to essays or written questionaires either to support or reinforce interview data. Such approaches are sometimes claimed to be less intimidating for children but may also have limited value for those with poor literacy skills.

- Can we accurately interpret what pupils say?

It is a challenge for any interviewer to ensure that their interpretation of the spoken word is accurate, particularly when transcribing the spoken word to paper. The loss of body language and intimation that can result from such transcription is an important consideration. It was certainly a challenge for me to analyse and present the pupils' perspectives in a written form that maintained their own accounts yet also introduced additional interpretation and comment.

- Can we expect children to accurately recall past events?

The extent to which children can be expected to accurately recall situations and events from the past and whether any accounts that rely on memory may become somewhat distorted, is an important consideration. It is possible that pupils forget or repress certain thoughts or are reluctant to express certain feelings or perspectives. I am aware that using interviewing as a methodological technique certainly makes a basic assumption that pupils want to talk, can articulate their thoughts, and can remember events accurately from their past. Such assumptions may place extremely high expectations on the pupils and may be unrealistic. In addition, although few pupils in the present study were openly reluctant to be interviewed, it is very likely that they carefully selected the information they felt prepared to share. Issues of confidentiality and trust are very hard to overcome in a brief interview and may affect the nature of the data collected.

I did find a few pupils who openly expressed a reluctance or inability to share thoughts or perspectives. John, a 13 year old pupil at Southdown who had been statemented as a result of continued disruptive and aggressive behaviour both at school and at home, and who had been receiving psychiatric treatment, had stopped one avenue of discussion regarding his family life with the comment:

"Well that's getting personal isn't it?"

Wayne was a 16 year old boy who was attending the Oakwood Centre. He had been referred following psychiatric treatment and the experience of severe social problems (bullying) in mainstream school. He had subsequently displayed disruptive and aggressive behaviours both at home and at school, and had finally refused to attend school. He was prepared to admit that his memory was somewhat selective, stating:

"I've got a good memory for some things and a bad memory for some things, especially things that I don't like to remember. I find it difficult to remember because I blotted it out."

He continued later by saying:

"I don't wanna remember anything about school so I never do ... there are some things but I just don't wanna talk about them. I can't remember specific incidents very well. I can remember some things if I think very hard."

Interestingly, a few pupils expressed a state of confusion in their minds when trying to answer interview questions. Susan, a withdrawn and shy 14 year old girl, referred to the Oakwood Centre by her psychiatrist, who had experienced major turmoil and trauma in her home life and had demonstrated acute paranoia and anxiety in a mainstream school, stated:

"I can't remember very far back, I get mixed up."

Robert, a 13 year old boy, also referred to the Oakwood Centre following psychiatric treatment, was almost totally unable to describe past experiences, particularly at home. He explained quietly that he had no recall of his father being at home before the break up of his parents' marriage or of his father leaving the home. Robert was a school refuser, saying very little during his days at the Centre and reluctant to talk openly during interviews.

- ## Are all pupils' voices represented?

At Southdown a number of boys were unavailable for interview. Such pupils were regularly absent from school, or had been suspended and removed from classes, and should be considered as significant lost voices. It is important to recognise that in research of this nature results may be based on the words of more articulate respondents, from whom the bulk of the data is acquired and may therefore be distorted. The articulate respondents may also provide further distortion by their eagerness to please the researcher, or to say what they think the researcher wishes to hear. It would not be surprising to find pupils who have been conditioned in classrooms to give the 'correct' answers, trying very hard to do the same in an interview situation!

- ## Can we find a truly representative group of interviewees?

As with any relatively small research project I am aware that the representativeness of my pupil sample may have been limited. Although the interviews involved a reasonable cross section of behaviours typical of pupils with EBD, the sample did not include the perspective of many girls, nor minority racial or ethnic groups.

- ## Does the nature of the relationship with the researcher influence a pupil's responses?

The opportunity to build a relationship with a pupil prior to interviewing may or may not encourage a pupil to talk freely. Obviously if the researcher works in the school there is a possibility that their relationship may be a negative one! I held the role of Teacher in Charge at the Oakwood Centre and am aware that this may have given me a different type of relationship with the children in that setting compared to my role at Southdown where I was a supply teacher. However, I believe that familiarity with the pupils was of benefit to my data collection in both settings.

- **Does a series of interviews over a period of time influence pupils' responses?**

Pupils at the Oakwood Centre may have offered somewhat different perspectives to the boys at Southdown School for two main reasons. Firstly, most gave a series of interviews over a period of one year as opposed to just one interview, offering me a greater opportunity for building rapport with them than a one off interview. Secondly, these pupils may have had the opportunity to reflect on their experiences between interviews and therefore offer increasingly insightful data.

- **How do children who are familiar with therapeutic interaction respond to interviewing?**

It seemed to me that the pupils who have been involved in extensive therapeutic 'conversation' prior to the interviews with me did respond somewhat differently to others. Many of the pupils at the Oakwood Centre had been through therapeutic treatment programmes prior to attending the Centre, and I felt this to have affected the ability of some of them to interpret factors and events relating to their own behaviour. The extent to which these therapeutic interventions had created or helped shape their views and perspectives and their interpretation of events is difficult to determine yet important to acknowledge. Pupils having undergone therapy appeared in certain cases to talk more freely and with greater analytical insight of their experiences and behaviour.

- **How do pupils perceive the interview process?**

Many pupils appeared honoured and somewhat surprised to have been given the opportunity to talk, and this honour was enhanced by the use of a tape machine and my disclosure that I would be hoping to write a book about them! Yet no matter how skilful my questioning, and how informal the relationship I built, a pupil's boundaries were his or her own. They appeared to have made their own judgements regarding the nature and extent of the information they considered it appropriate to share and this was unpredictable. Roy, a 14 year old boy who had been referred to the Oakwood Centre by a psychiatrist who had been working with him on his anxiety and school phobia, stated that he found it easy to talk in the interview but:

"It depends what mood I'm in ... If I'm in a happy mood it's OK."

One pupil Neil, who was a 12 year old boy attending Southdown School as a result of his aggression with peers and disruptive and disturbing behaviours in a mainstream school, openly described his very own personal goal for the interview. He stated angrily that:

"I want the Headteacher to hear this, what I'm saying."

As he spoke he appeared to be releasing all of his anger and frustration onto the tape and clearly saw a purpose for the tape beyond that of the research.

23

He was anxious to have his own copy and for everyone else to hear what he had to say!

- **Is research based on interviewing children manipulative and unethical?**

Anyone using interviewing to gain research data should question the true rights of the participants they interview, particularly when they are children and school pupils. We should be aware of the potential vulnerability of interviewees in certain research situations particularly concerning the degree of control that they have over the information they disclose. Researchers should question how honest they are being with questioning and admit to the somewhat manipulative use of questioning commonly used to get interviewees to talk and disclose information that even they themselves may not be aware they are disclosing.

- **When interviewing children in schools is the quality of data affected by any simple, practical problems?**

Finding the time to complete interviews can be difficult at times, and negotiations with teachers for pupils to leave classrooms have to be made using sensitivity and tact. Finding a quiet, private space in which to conduct interviews can also pose problems. Interruptions are common and privacy frequently lacking. The implications of these difficulties are hard to judge, but may possibly inhibit certain pupils and reduce their willingness to disclose certain thoughts and perspectives.

Finally, tape-recording the pupils may impact their willingness to disclose information as the tape recorder can daunt some pupils, although others apparently ignore it or soon forget it.

3 How we see it:

The children's perceptions of the factors that influenced their behaviour

In this chapter I have focused on the factors and processes that were perceived to have significantly influenced the behaviour of the pupils who were interviewed. It is presented in three sections:

3.1 The schools and the teachers.

3.2 Family, sociocultural and socioeconomic factors.

3.3 Factors associated with the individual pupil's psychology and physiology.

I started the interviews with the belief that any attempt to better understand pupils with EBD and their behaviour should involve an exploration of all factors that may interact and influence this behaviour. As I explained in chapter 1 the various theories of behaviour encourage different foci within educational research. The extent to which a researcher elects to explore certain factors that may influence pupils' behaviour is likely to be dependent on his or her particular theoretical beliefs. For example, previous studies have focused specifically on factors linked to schooling, some on the family or socioeconomic background and others on past experiences and psychodynamics. Amongst them some have specifically utilised pupil perceptions to achieve their goal. However, as Blythe & Milner (1994) state; '... there is a need for further investigation of the identification and interaction of relevant factors' (p296) and other researchers have echoed these beliefs. Faupel (1990) for example, is quoted in Barrow (1995), as stating; 'Understanding problem behaviour will not be found by focussing on the child, nor by focussing on the school, but in the study and analysis of the *interaction between them*.' (p52).

The research on which this book is based attempted to use the perceptions of pupils with EBD to illustrate the relative significance of all possible factors that may have impacted the pupils' behaviour. I attempted not only to explore the pupils' own view of the internal, psychological or physiological factors that they perceived as influencing their behaviours, but also the factors belonging to the various systems impacting their lives, such as school and family life. As Armstrong et al (1993) state; 'The disturbing behaviour of children may arise from tensions in the home or school, as well as from personality or constitutional "disorders".' (p128). Certain publications have criticised research that has focused too closely on single factors. For example, Pasternicki, Wake-

Factors Affecting Behaviour

Different theories encourage focus on different factors.

The interaction of significant factors is important.

A Systemic Approach to Behaviour

It is important to avoid focusing on single factors or systems.

Factors within different systems may be perceived by children as influencing their behaviour.

field, Robertson & Edwards (1993) describe research that has investigated single factors relating to truancy, rather than seeking to explore the broader complexity of the reasons behind such behaviour. They state; '...the research studies examined the influence of a single possible causal factor rather than the interaction between a number of possible factors.' (p3).

I hope that the three sections of this chapter provide you, the reader, with the opportunity to benefit and learn from the results of my unique enquiry into the importance of all possible influential factors on pupils' behaviour, using the pupils' own viewpoint. In each of the three sections I offer you a combination of relevant literature in the field, increased understanding of the theories behind the behaviour of children with EBD and enhanced knowledge of the various factors that affect pupils' behaviour. I have presented the pupils' perspectives using their own words wherever possible, accompanied by my own analysis and interpretation to illustrate the significance of their statements. The initial contribution made by each pupil is accompanied by a brief outline of his or her age and background. This is intended to give you some insight into the problems that each pupil had experienced and to be better able to assess the significance of their statements. (A few of the pupils have already been introduced in chapter 2). The names of the schools and of all pupils have been changed to ensure anonymity.

3.1 **The schools and the teachers**

A large percentage of the interview data collected from pupils was concerned with the role of schools and schooling factors in contributing to their behaviour and difficulties. The whole experience of schools and schooling and the various social and educational processes occurring within the mainstream schools that the pupils had attended, were clearly of significance for the pupils in relation to their behaviour and their subsequent placement in a special school. The results presented in this section offer powerful support to currently developing beliefs that schools themselves may actually contribute to a pupil's problems. The previous decade has opened the doors of research into what constitutes effective schooling and the results presented here reinforce much of this research. Such research has helped reveal the nature of an effective school that meets the needs of all of its pupils, including those displaying disturbing behaviour. The pupils with EBD interviewed in this study were certainly able to reveal the important role that they perceived their mainstream schools to have played in contributing to their difficulties.

Cooper et al (1994) give extensive details of research that has been carried out in this field, including that from the USA and Australia. They draw from various sources to make important and far reaching statements including that; 'The institutional arrangements in schools have a profound influence on the social and emotional adjustment of their students and that schools have it in their power to inhibit, or exacerbate, the development of emotional and behavioural difficulties and to function as effective therapeutic agents.' (p173). Kreft (1993) traces the evolution of school effectiveness research. Interestingly, he reports that although in 1966 the Coleman Report stated that schools themselves do make a difference, most research at that time was still focusing on the impact of socioeconomic factors on pupil achievement in school and not on the possible impact of schooling processes themselves. Kreft (1993) refers to a second generation of research that has considered the schools themselves to be highly significant in providing either effective or ineffective experiences for their pupils and describes this research as no longer regarding schools as '… the black box in which something goes in and something comes out.' (p105). Such research has gone some way towards changing attitudes to schools and this is well described in a quote by Tyerman cited in O'Keeffe & Stoll (1995) who refers to the '…fatally flawed psychology of years ago, which viewed school as an unproblematic good and anyone who recoiled from it as *ipso facto* deficient, or deviant or even proto criminal.' (p10). However, O'Keeffe & Stoll also suggest that things may not have changed greatly and they comment that certain people in positions of power still turn to the children themselves or their sociocultural backgrounds as being at fault:

> 'Sad to say, this outlook is still apparent among many politicians and administrators. Either they regard children as possessing a disfigured psychology, or, if they do take a sociological perspective, this is solely in relation to childrens' bad homes etc.' (p10).

Nevertheless, much previous research has revealed very tangible aspects of the school itself that may adversely affect pupil behaviour and social relationships, and the results of this research cannot be overlooked or ignored. Such work includes Hargreaves (1967), Rutter, Maughan, Mortimore and Ouston (1979), Galloway & Goodwin (1987) and Reynolds & Cuttance (1992). The work of these researchers revealed that the behaviour of individual pupils could not simply be attributed to social background, defective homes, or psychological damage through previous experiences. The role of the school itself was also important. In addition, this research began to reveal the importance of less tangible aspects of schooling which have become known as the ethos of the establishment, and have also led to an interest in the social aspects of schooling for pupils. This sociological research has revealed a better understanding of the pupils' experience in terms of subcultures and groups which exist in schools, (Woods, 1980,1990), and the behaviour which is associated with such groups. The pupils I describe in this book certainly made a significant number of comments concerning social interaction in schools and reinforce the important impact of social processes within schools on behaviour.

In contrast to those who pursue school effectiveness research with a strong belief that it may ultimately provide the answers to our problems in helping pupils with EBD, Angus (1993) offers some alternative views concerning the role of school in the creation or maintenance of disturbing behaviours. He reviews three books concerned with school effectiveness and criticises those who he describes as being obsessed with school effect, considering that they are, or have been, ignoring wider social issues. He states that they have a '…limited view of context…' (p341). He continues by saying that those researching school effectiveness are not considering an '…interactive relationship between schools, culture and society…' (p342). Clearly it is important that we do not allow school effectiveness research to overshadow the important impact of social background on behaviour, possibly giving policy makers the opportunity to place all responsibility for the behaviour of pupils with EBD on the schools and their teachers.

Some continue to doubt the role of the school when children experience difficulties.

Schools and Behaviour

There are tangible aspects of the schooling experience that can adversely affect pupils' success.

Less tangible social aspects of schooling, including the ethos can also impact pupil behaviour.

Placing the Blame on Schools

Too much concern with school effectiveness may be considered to overshadow other significant factors.

In this section I have presented the results from my interviews that refer specifically to school and schooling factors. For clarity the results are presented as four subsections;

- Size of the schools, classes and teacher to pupil ratio.

- Teachers and teaching.

- The curriculum.

- Social problems.

3.1 (i) Size of the schools, classes, and teacher to pupil ratio

A significant number of pupils who were interviewed commented on how the size of their schools and classes had influenced their behaviours and feelings about school. The perceptions of the pupils who commented on this issue were particularly interesting because they varied in the actual way in which school or class size manifested itself as problems and impacted their ability to remain in a mainstream setting.

Size and nature of school buildings

The Affect of the Size and Structure of School Buildings

The size and physical structure of the school buildings can affect pupils who refuse to attend and who experience phobias, depression or physical illness.

Six of the pupils interviewed described a fear resulting from their subjective view of the size of the school buildings, and their institutional nature. This was a problem particularly for pupils who had entered special education as a result of poor attendance or school refusal. Phobia, physical illness, and depression were commonly diagnosed for these pupils and psychiatric treatment prior to special education had been provided in certain cases. Pupils described various aspects of the physical nature of the schools that symbolised their institutional nature, and were perceived as having contributed to their fears. For example when Robert was asked why he had become scared of school, he replied:

> "Corridors probably...there was one long corridor that went through the whole school."

Wayne had a different yet equally vivid perception of his school:

> "The school seemed to have a cage round it."

Sarah, was a 13 year old girl attending the Oakwood Centre following psychiatric treatment for suicidal thoughts and school phobia. She had refused to go to school soon after transferring to the secondary setting and she was one pupil from those interviewed whose perceptions of the school buildings were recounted when she tried to describe the root of her difficulties:

> "...it's a hard school to get on with, it's too big. I can't see how any of them cope with it that size. So I used to stand in the corridor, I used to look ahead, and the corridor used to be... honestly you could put a train tunnel down it, it was miles. I used to stand there with all these girls crowding around me and I used to say 'where the hell am I, what

am I doing here?' All the corridors used to look black. It was too big for me. I couldn't cope with it. I used to burst out crying in lessons."

Interestingly, it seems that such perceptions are not unusual amongst many mainstream school pupils preparing for the transition from the primary to the secondary setting. Measor & Woods (1984) interviewed a number of pupils at that stage in their school careers and found expressions about being frightened, worried, scared and nervous, quite common and in association with comments on the size of the new school they were to enter. Their pupils stated fears of losing their way in 'the maze of corridors and classrooms.' (p9).

Roy was clearly able to recall his experiences concerning the fear of getting lost. He described both the size and institutional nature of the building:

"I kept getting lost a lot. It was a massive school and I kept getting lost."

"It seemed I was small, you had buildings two storeys high everywhere, and all your bigger people all around you."

"The size of the buildings and the dangers in them too. Corridors, ledges, stairs, doors."

He felt he was ill prepared for the transition from primary to secondary school:

"The primary schools don't prepare you for the change to secondary, the size. I think it would have helped if I knew what I was walking into. I was squashed in the corridors."

Lengthy interview time with both Roy and Sarah revealed many other factors that they associated with their difficulties in addition to these perceptions of the school. It would however appear that unlike the pupils in Measor & Woods' (1984) study for whom the fear of transition was an understandable yet passing fear, these two pupils did not move through their fear. Instead it had developed and contributed to a more complex web of difficulties and as the interviews showed, these particular perceptions had remained with them as a significant contributory factor in their mainstream schooling difficulties. The comments made by Roy appear to suggest an enhanced feeling of insecurity and awareness of danger, which may typify the perceptions of certain pupils with EBD.

Adding to the data that suggests the importance of school size as a significant factor linked to these pupils' difficulties are the comments made by a small number of pupils regarding their experience of the special school setting. For these pupils the success of their alternative placement or special school and its appropriateness for their needs was closely related to the small size and less institutionalised nature of the school building, which had made their attendance easier:

"The building, no long corridors, human."

"I liked the size of it."

Making School Transitions

Moving from primary to secondary school appears to create anxiety.

The Complexity of Pupils With EBD

Pupils who develop EBD may have enhanced feelings of anxiety and insecurity in the school.

Special Schools

The success of a special school may be partly a result of its smaller size and less institutionalised nature.

Secondary Schools

Too many pupils in one building may create an intimidating environment for some vulnerable children who can go on to develop EBD.

For pupils such as Sarah and Roy, their difficulties had become more apparent on transfer to the secondary setting. This suggests that it is important to consider the major differences between the physical nature of the secondary and primary school settings as being a significant factor in the inability of certain pupils to make a successful transition. Associated with these physical differences between the primary and the secondary school buildings and possibly even dictating their existence, is the difference in the number of pupils being educated in these two schools with secondary schools traditionally educating larger numbers of pupils in one building. Do these numbers create the need for institutionalised, intimidating school buildings that can lead to an unsuccessful transition and then develop into the more complex problem behaviours associated with the student with EBD? To summarise, the number of pupils being educated in one place inevitably influences the physical nature of the buildings, and for a minority of vulnerable children this becomes an important factor affecting their behaviour.

Size and social problems

Five pupils commented directly that the number of pupils in a school had contributed to their social problems. In addition to his comments regarding the physical nature of the school buildings, Wayne, expressed clear views that the large numbers of pupils in the mainstream school setting had contributed to his experiences of bullying and his subsequent problems in attending school:

Bullying

Large schools may increase the chances of bullying occurring.

> "The main thing about that school - miles too big. They couldn't keep an eye out for everybody."

Roy also commented on the number of pupils around him:

> "I couldn't walk across the playground without a squash. Everyone crowding around in gangs. Really packed out."

Supervision

Quality of supervision can be impaired when pupil numbers are high.

As Wayne's comment reveals, it was the inability of the staff to 'see' what was going on that was the problem for him. The sheer number of pupils in the secondary mainstream setting and high pupil/teacher ratios clearly left these pupils feeling vulnerable amongst their peers. Boulton (1993a) states from his studies on playground fighting that; 'Supervisors are often in charge of large numbers of children in the playground and the ratio may exceed 1:50.' (p199). Clearly vulnerability increases outside the classroom setting if this figure is accurate, and may support and justify the fears perceived by Wayne. He continued:

> "There's never anyone in charge around. There's always so many people at school, they're always flittering about, you can never get hold of them. It's like if you're getting hassle from anyone, you can't see anyone."

Another Oakwood Centre pupil Johnny, who was 12 years old and who had been expelled from a number of mainstream and special school placements as a result of aggressive and disruptive behaviours towards both staff and peers, also commented on the size of mainstream schools:

"They're all too big. When the teachers aren't there, they can't keep an eye on you. Too many kids and not enough teachers."

In addition to pupils perceiving there to be too few staff, Sarah also felt that staff were too busy to offer support in a large school:

"Teachers never have time in a big school."

Wayne added:

"No-one to talk to individually, and if you're getting bullied ... they can't sit and talk to you ... no individualisation."

In these statements pupils are clearly commenting on the quantity and quality of contact with teachers or members of staff. Whether this is in the classroom or outside it, the pupils' observations and subjective views bring up issues of a qualitative nature, such as relationships, which emerge from quantifiable factors such as numbers of teachers. Teachers are perceived as the means to safety and protection for those pupils who are vulnerable to the social life of the school, and certain pupils perceived this protection as inadequate both in quantity and quality. Johnny summed up his perception of why size makes a difference, when he commented on a positive aspect of the special school setting:

Relationships

The quality of pupil/teacher relationships may suffer in large schools.

"It's small, so if there's a little bit of trouble you can pounce straight away."

Roy explained his ability to attend the Oakwood Centre whilst failing in mainstream as:

"I feel safe here."

This feeling of safety appears to be linked to the pupils' perception of the physical nature of the school buildings and the number of pupils in the school. A small number of pupils in the study clearly suggested that reducing the number of pupils in schools would allow social problems between pupils to be reduced by making them more visible and manageable, or by improving the quality of relationships.

Special Schools

Some pupils describe feeling safer in a small school.

This problem of the lack of visibility of negative social interaction in the schools and its association with pupil numbers and ineffective classroom supervision or management was also perceived by certain pupils to extend into classroom situations. Karen was a 16 year old girl attending the Oakwood Centre. She had been referred for psychiatric treatment following severe social difficulties in the mainstream setting leading to school refusal and also aggression within the family. She explained:

"Having thirty people in a class, teacher can't keep an eye on everyone."

Practical subjects appeared to offer excellent opportunities for bullying, where large classes were perceived as preventing teachers either seeing problems or

31

dealing with them. George was a 16 year old Oakwood Centre pupil who had suffered a great deal of bullying in the schools he had previously attended. He had been referred to the Centre following his placement in a Children's Home as a result of family difficulties. He described his experiences in a CDT class:

> "Well, whilst he was helping someone else ... all the other lot would start throwing compasses and everything. If I'd go and tell Mr. Jenkins he'd just say 'Oh well, ignore them'. It got to one time where I just walked out of the classroom."

Karen generally perceived lessons as being the 'safest' part of her school day, often dreading and attempting to avoid the less structured periods such as break-times. As Cullingford (1993a) states; 'The classroom can even become a refuge in times of stress.' (p57). However, Karen described certain practical classes as creating opportunities for bullying and feelings of vulnerability:

> "Food studies was the worse, cause we had all the cookers around, and you couldn't see if anything was going on."

She continued:

> "Science was where I was having a lot of problems... I had acid thrown at me."

Physical Education classes were also mentioned by a number of the interviewees. Six of the pupils perceived this particular subject as creating opportunity for negative interaction. George related the problems he experienced to the number of pupils being taught together:

> "And cause of all the kids, if you were playing football, they'd try and deliberately trip you up and throw the ball at you and bundle you."

Obviously such behaviour within classrooms can be associated with a number of variables, not only class size, but Cullingford (1993a) considers that large numbers of people in the confined spaces of the school environment can affect relationships in a negative way. He states; 'Many of the relationships, in such confined spaces, are volatile.' (p59). For some pupils, escaping from that confinement was a difficult thing to achieve. The highly social nature of the schools and the lack of provision for quiet, individual time were problems for Sarah:

> "I made myself a prefect because I didn't want to go outside and play with them .... so I didn't have to go out and play with everyone else. It was really a way of escaping and getting help."

Wayne also wanted to escape from social contact:

> "I asked the teachers if they would put me in isolation, so I'd go up the hall, do all my work."

Harris (1994) deduces from her interviews with pupils in a mainstream setting that; 'It is difficult to be alone, an individual - for most of the time students

Classroom Safety

Pupils can feel unsafe in large classes with ineffective classroom supervision.

Practical subjects and PE appear to create the most problems.

Escaping

Some pupils need and seek ways to escape or avoid social contact.

are seen as part of a group ...' (p63). Perhaps some of the pupils with EBD who were interviewed in this study reveal an enhanced vulnerability to this expectation to be socially involved and group orientated at all times.

Interestingly, the social vulnerability and the fear of social contact experienced by these pupils with EBD which they perceived as being associated with the physical nature of the school, the number of pupils both in and out of classes, coupled with inadequate staff 'protection', does not support some of the major research on bullying that has been published. Based on his extensive Norwegian studies, in a recent article Olweus (1994) states; 'There were no positive associations between level of bully/victim problems (the percentage of bullied and/or bullying students) and school or class size.' (p1177), although he admits that his research does in fact contrast with commonly held public views. He claims that '...the size of the class or school appears to be of negligible importance for the relative frequency or level of bully/victim problems' yet he goes on to say; 'It is, nevertheless, a fact that absolute number of bullied and bullying students is greater on average in big schools and in big classes.' (p1177).

Research

Some research doubts the link between school size and bullying.

An important focus of much of the recent research on bullying is the somewhat intangible and illusive 'school ethos' which is believed to be a factor influencing aggressive social behaviour. It is generally believed that the ethos of the school can influence the attitudes and relationships of the people within it. Scherer et al (1990), believe that the school effectiveness research of the 1970's and 1980's regarding the importance of the physical aspects of the school are '...not as important as the less tangible aspects, or ethos, of the school.' (p14). Such a statement is surprising as it suggests that the ethos of a school is separable from the physical aspects of school and class size. If ethos is considered to be the school's social climate or atmosphere then it is surely inseparable from the number of pupils within the school or its classrooms, and the resulting physical nature or requirements of the buildings. Significantly, the pupils in this study raised all of these factors as being associated with their behaviours. Effective pastoral care is generally considered to be a valuable contribution to the correct 'ethos' of a school, yet Reid, Hopkins & Holly (1987) ask; 'Is pastoral care equally effective in year groups of 250 compared with those of 75, 125 or 150?' (p79). In other words, research which reveals the importance of the ethos of a school in contributing to that school's effectiveness, must continue to look at the close link between this ethos and the potential impact of school and class size on its positive development. The two issues appear to be inseparable.

School Ethos

School ethos is believed to impact behaviour and may be closely linked to size of schools and classes.

Size and discipline

A further aspect of the importance of school and class size to the difficulties experienced by pupils with EBD in the mainstream setting lies with their perceptions of discipline. For a number of the pupils interviewed for this study, the way in which they had been disciplined and the discipline procedures within their mainstream schools, were perceived as having contributed in a variety of ways to their problems within that setting. Harris (1994) makes an interesting statement from her research, which brings discipline procedures into the debate on school/class size. 'The size of the population and the confined space justified in some teachers' eyes, the need for the strict and highly visible discipline regime...' (p 61).

Discipline Techniques

Large schools and classes can result in teachers resorting to using ineffective methods of discipline concerned with control.

Pye (1988) pursues the idea that much of the need for punishment and discipline results from the fact that classes are too large. He claims that teachers worry about controlling large classes, become stressed and insecure, and this insecurity leads to less effective interaction with the pupils. He claims that; 'Smaller numbers would multiply parental relationships between teachers and pupils' (p165), and that in large classes the teachers' power 'to perceive individuality and complexity in pupils dies.' (p166). He also claims that teachers' insecurity is transferred to the pupils and they too become insecure. Overall he suggests that teachers become referees in the classroom. The size of the school may also be reflected in the content and nature of a school policy on discipline. Harris (1994) notes; 'The size of the school's population has been of increasing concern to senior management mainly because of the pressures that such numbers place on simply "managing" the population let alone maintaining an adequate teaching and learning environment.' (p61).

Pupils described ineffective and frustrating methods of discipline that they perceived as having done nothing to help or alleviate the problems that they had been experiencing, nor to change their behaviour. Wayne described the impersonal, ineffective nature of the discipline he experienced:

> "I got thousands of detentions. People'd have a go at me, I'd tell 'em to shut up and have a go at them. I'd get told off for talking. I'd usually get detention for that. We'd get things called microlines. They'd go off and have a cup of tea ... and they'd leave you and you'd never get a chance to tell your side of the story."

George described the lack of effectiveness of impersonal mass disciplining which appears to be adopted by many large secondary schools:

Ineffective Classroom Discipline

Certain discipline techniques and approaches do nothing to change behaviour in the long term.

> "If you're naughty you get a little pink slip... take it to the Head's office, and it goes on your file. If you get six you get suspended. If you get eight you get expelled. I used to flush them down the toilet. They never checked up."

Other pupils also perceived the discipline as uncaring and impersonal, including Johnny who described his experiences:

> "He gave me a punishment. Stay in the library and do your work. I was there for about two or three hours and he didn't even come back in three hours. I just walked out. They just don't care, do they?"

Some pupils praised teachers who knew them or their needs as individuals:

> "She gets to know you, to know what you want."

> "Well listening and how she copes with you ... everybody's different."

A pupil interviewed by Pye (1988) felt that smaller classes would allow pupils and teachers to relate to each other better 'as people, as human beings.' (p168). Sarah felt that teachers in special schools did try to build relationships, perhaps reinforcing Pye's belief that both teachers and pupils feel safer with the smaller numbers of pupils in the special school:

"Teachers are willing to listen to your problems, don't alienate you. Like in mainstream you're there to learn and that's that really."

The extent to which these forms of discipline and their perceived ineffectiveness is a consequence of large numbers of pupils in schools and classes is obviously open to debate. However, some pupils clearly felt that the approach adopted in the smaller special school was more effective. Colin was a 14 year old pupil at Southdown School who had displayed highly disturbing behaviours within the mainstream setting, and been referred to Southdown for education and also to a counsellor for therapeutic support. In the interview he tried to articulate the differences between the approach of the mainstream school and the special setting in terms of discipline:

"Southdown School has been kind. In mainstream you do one thing wrong, chuck something or swear at a teacher, you'd be automatically suspended. At this school you can do things hundreds and hundreds of times and you still don't get kicked out because they want to talk through your problems. They want to talk to you about it, and see if they can fix it for you."

Andy at the Oakwood Centre was a 14 year old boy who had been removed from mainstream school for disruptive behaviour and truancy. He made an interesting comment that perhaps helps to explain the subtle differences between this and the special school:

"More relaxed. The atmosphere. In a mainstream school there's tension in the air. In a school like this there's no tension at all."

Interestingly the special school provisions with their smaller pupil numbers were not perceived to have achieved greater success in terms of discipline by adopting stricter regimes, but by showing a more personal caring approach where justice could more clearly be seen to be done. As Gerry explained:

"At this school there is discipline when you've done something wrong, you can actually see when you've done something wrong."

William was a 13 year old school refuser attending Southdown School, who had learning difficulties and had been bullied within the mainstream setting. He expressed similar sentiments:

"This school is really caring for people's needs where mainstream they would say do this, do that and do this, and tough luck if you've got a disability, otherwise you get an hours detention."

Laslett (1995) thoughtfully takes discipline and its potential association with school or class size into the area of relationships within schools. He refers to the staff who worked in the early special schools and how they knew that:

Relationships with Teachers

Pupils feel their individual needs are often unrecognised in the mainstream schools.

Discipline In Special Schools

Smaller facilities offering specialised provision can allow for a more effective personalised approach to discipline.

35

'...a reliance on punishing children militated against the goals of the schools and against the kind of relationships with children which the staff knew to be beneficial. They realised that punishment is a more complicated and potentially a more destructive intervention than those who advocate it realise.' (p6).

Obviously the question here concerns the extent to which this more relaxed, possibly individualised caring approach is possible in a large school. Ken, a 15 year old boy attending Southdown who had been in trouble for aggressive, disruptive behaviour in mainstream school, simply pleaded for a more understanding and personalised discipline system. He stated that all he wanted was:

"Someone to just listen to me really."

He described one teacher who helped him:

"When I was in trouble she used to come down and sit with me and talk."

Previous research has shown that pupils are quite able to recognise a need for discipline but are also clear as to what they consider to be effective. Quicke (1994) in referring to previous studies of pupils' perspectives states that pupils; '...recognised the need for a disciplinary framework,' (p105), but one which they expected to be exercised in a non-authoritarian and non-coercive way. When discipline does not conform to these standards it may be seen to add to pupil difficulties. Gerry was a 14 year old boy attending the Oakwood Centre. He had severe learning difficulties that had resulted in a special education placement but had also been expelled from both day and residential special schools following disturbing behaviours and truancy. He clearly saw the nature of the discipline at a previous school as exacerbating his behaviour problems:

"No school needs to be strict. When I was in 'X' school, I was so naughty ... and they had discipline there. It just makes you do more naughty stuff."

Karen, explained the potential role of discipline procedures in offering the opportunity to increase peer group status and self esteem:

"Some children like to be told off ... I'm like big and cool."

Stevenson & Ellsworth (1991) describe certain punishments as 'counter productive', quoting a pupil they had interviewed in a USA survey of truants as saying 'like giving candy to a baby ...first I skipped, then they kicked me out.' (p284). They suggest that 'suspension for truancy "punishes" a student by ensuring that the behaviour being punished continues.' (p283).

Discipline Backfiring

Ineffective discipline can create more problems than it solves.

In this present study, Danny, a 14 year old boy at Southdown School with learning difficulties and a history of disruption and truancy, clearly described how he used the school rules to his own advantage:

"I wanted to get chucked out ... so I just mucked about everyday and didn't do my detentions."

It is possible to suggest from this type of statement that the impersonal discipline methods used in many mainstream schools may be insufficient and inadequate for the pupil with EBD who requires more time and patience on an individual basis. Such methods of discipline may even be used by the pupils to their own advantage. There may also be significant negative consequences for the ethos of the school and the relationships within it which result from ineffective discipline methods. In turn, the adoption of these methods is strongly bound to pupil numbers both in the schools and in the classrooms. In summary, if it is these numbers which dictate discipline methods, and the resulting spin-offs in terms of ethos and relationships, then we are considering class and school size as a significant factor related to the effectiveness of mainstream schools to help pupils with EBD.

Size and academic problems

Of a more tangible nature than the effect of school and class size on the social interactions and relationships in a school may be its effect on the pupils' learning and academic progress. On this issue, the pupils' perceptions clearly suggested that being in classes that they considered to have contained too many pupils had certainly influenced their lack of academic progress and their unacceptable behaviour. As previously described, some major research reveals that class size is not influential on pupils' progress, yet, an NFER Study (Times Educational Supplement, 1995) involving two hundred and sixty five primary school heads, revealed that nearly 60% of them said that their Key Stage 2 classes were too big to enable adequate teaching of the national curriculum. Eleven of the pupils interviewed in the present study supported this finding and directly described how they felt that they had not had sufficient help from teachers. Six boys at Southdown School made comments illustrating this point:

"Too many people in the class, you have to wait and by the time teacher gets to you, time's run out."

"Too many people in a class, and you don't get the kind of help you need."

"In mainstream school if you get stuck on a sum you may have to wait ages and ages and ages, 'cause there's like thirty two people in a class."

"There was only one teacher and a class of thirty six kids, it was too much."

"Because there's about thirty of them in a class and it's hard to concentrate 'cause there's only one teacher."

"Too big a school for me to cope with, probably didn't get enough attention."

Discipline and Pupils with EBD

Class and school size may result in ineffective methods of discipline for children with EBD who require a more personalised approach to their behaviours.

Pupils with EBD appear to require more time and patience than some mainstream school discipline policies provide.

Getting Enough Support

Pupils perceive that their academic progress is impeded by lack of teacher support.

The consequences of large class sizes for these pupils and of having received inadequate help with their work were varied. Boredom, frustration and humiliation were all described as arising within classrooms, with sometimes highly destructive behaviour resulting. (See chapter 4). 'Messing about' was a term used by a number of the pupils to describe their own behaviour. Johnny, at the Oakwood Centre, who did not find academic work easy, and had been expelled from mainstream school, stated:

> "I mess about if I can't do the work. I can't do the work and none of the teachers helped me, so I'd just mess about."

He clearly perceived his teachers as not helping him, although it would be interesting to be able to assess the extent to which help was offered but was still perceived to be inadequate, particularly considering that at the Oakwood Centre Johnny required almost constant one to one tuition. However, his perceptions of 'none of the teachers helped' is similar to the feelings of Ken at Southdown, another boy who perceived himself as being 'ignored' in a class that was too big:

Impact on Behaviour

Lack of academic support can lead to misbehaviour.

> "I think it was because I was getting ignored in my class, 'cause it was such a big class and I just wanted help and they just ignored me the teachers. I just started messing about and the teachers sent me out of the room."

The behavioural problems for pupils finding inadequate classroom support in large classes is significant and will be discussed in more detail in chapter 4. Additionally, further analysis of how the pupils perceived the demands of the curriculum and their teachers as significant problems in addition to the effects of large class size will be developed in following sections.

Key points emerging from this section

- The pupils' comments suggest that the size of a school and the classes they attend do make a difference to their behaviour.

- Reducing school and class sizes may help minimise school failure for certain pupils.

- The results of qualitative studies may clash with those of empirical study when determining the effect of school and class size on school effectiveness.

- School and class size impacts the ethos of a school and ethos has been recognised as an important aspect of school effectiveness.

- Pupils with EBD may have different needs from those children who succeed in the mainstream setting.

- Pupils with EBD may suffer more significantly in large schools and classes owing to the greater complexity of their needs.

Thoughts for your reflection

- What are your views regarding how your own school and class sizes may be impacting the behaviour of certain children?

- Are you fully aware of some of the frustrations and anxieties that being in a large school or class can create for your pupils?

- Based on the statements made by the pupils in this section, are there any steps you could take in your own school or classroom to reduce feelings of insecurity or isolation and to ensure that the needs of all pupils are being met?

- Can you create a sense of belonging and warmth in your school or classroom even when large numbers of pupils are involved?

Tips for improving your success with difficult or challenging children

- Be vigilant and caring at all times when children are around you, even when you may not be the one primarily responsible.

- Take every opportunity to build relationships with children by letting them talk to you.

- Be aware of your pupils' behaviour in all parts of your classroom, including hidden areas.

- Provide opportunities and areas for pupils to have respite and a break from other children.

- Try to manage behaviour and use discipline techniques that show that you care about the individuals involved.

- Give difficult pupils the opportunity to talk to you and problem solve together.

- Explore ways of providing efficient and effective help to all pupils in your classroom, even when the class is large.

3.1 (ii) **Teachers and teaching**

A number of pupils in this study perceived teachers' personalities, skills and styles as factors having contributed to their problems within the mainstream setting. When describing 'in school' factors which had either created or added to their difficulties, their teachers frequently took criticism and blame. Fontana (1984) has similarly stressed the importance of teachers and their behaviours on pupils' success in school, stating that '...more attention paid to the social environment in which children learn, and in particular to that environment as represented by teacher behaviours, will lead to pupil learning that is more efficient and effective.' (p114).

Some of the specific issues arising from the pupils' perceptions and relating to teachers and teaching and their impact on the behaviour of pupils with EBD are developed in the following pages.

Discipline and control

One issue that consistently emerged during interviews and is frequently described in similar studies (Munn, Johnson & Holligan, 1990), is the nature and success of the discipline and control techniques adopted by teachers. Julie was a 16 year old girl attending the Oakwood Centre as a result of school refusal following difficulties with academic work. She stated clearly that a good teacher was one who:

> "Can keep the class under control."

Controlling the Class

Pupils want teachers to be in control in the classroom.

Interestingly, pupils were often frustrated by an apparent lack of discipline including Rick and Simon who were both 16 year old boys attending Southdown School having been expelled from mainstream schools for delinquent, aggressive and disruptive behaviours in addition to truancy. They made interesting comments about how inadequate discipline from teachers and the school itself may have been partly to blame for the problems they had experienced in mainstream school:

> "I blame partly myself, but the teachers have got to take some of the blame. They let me get away with murder."

> "The school shouldn't have let me get away with some of the things that I shouldn't have done."

These statements illustrate the importance of appropriate and effective use of discipline by teachers for certain pupils with EBD.

Other pupils made clear statements regarding the forms of discipline that they had experienced and one method of control that was considered unacceptable by a considerable number of pupils was shouting. Eleven of the pupils interviewed mentioned shouting as a negative behaviour or strategy for teachers to use as a form of discipline. For Robert, the experience of being shouted at in front of his peers was perceived as particularly disturbing:

> "He was shouting at me right in front of the class and I was embarrassed."

Teachers Shouting

Many pupils with EBD do not like teachers who shout.

Two other pupils also commented with more general statements:

> "I didn't like the teachers, they always used to shout at you."

> "They used to shout a lot. It's all they ever seemed to do, shout."

Cullingford (1993b) suggests that boys are shouted at more than girls and that the gender of the teacher may influence their discipline technique. Although this was not supported by a significant number of pupils in this study, one comment was made by Guy, a 14 year old boy with learning and language difficulties that appeared to have manifested themselves as behavioural difficulties within the mainstream setting. He stated:

> "I prefer lady teachers 'cause they're soft. They don't shout as often, like men, they really shout."

This dislike of shouting appears to be common to a number of previous studies including that reported in the Times Educational Supplement (1992) and others involving mainstream pupils. Interestingly however, Munn et al (1990) found mainstream pupils considered shouting by teachers when maintaining discipline as having both negative and positive outcomes. This was certainly not evident from the pupils with EBD.

For a small number of pupils the expectation that teachers should maintain control and discipline in the classroom was coupled with another requirement, which was that the teacher should also be able to retain control of him or her self! Susan, described the qualities of one teacher whom she 'liked':

> "He didn't shout, he only gets angry when he wants to make himself angry."

This statement appears to reinforce the view of Fontana (1986) who describes the importance of a teacher being able to '...observe her own emotional states.' (p167). He uses this statement in the context of explaining the importance of teachers refraining from imposing their moods on a class. Cullingford (1993a) also raises the issue of teachers' self control, stating; 'No children resent strictness but they do dislike the teacher who loses self-control'. (p59). Losing control may be exhibited when a teacher resorts to physical means of discipline, and such physical aggression by teachers towards pupils was something described by three of the pupils interviewed in this study. It was, not surprisingly, considered unacceptable to them as a means of control and discipline. Their comments were:

> "The teacher grabbed hold of me and threw me across the classroom."

> "Teacher got hold of my hair and pulled my head back."

> "He used to hold you, jolt you when he used to shout."

It was also of importance to pupils that any discipline or punishment used by teachers should fit whatever the 'crime' had been and certainly not exceed it. As one pupil suggested, a good teacher should be:

> ".... not too strict, or who can be strict but don't go over the limit, like tell you off for the slightest thing."

Teachers Controlling Themselves

Teachers should be in control of their own emotions.

Physical forms of discipline are unacceptable.

It was interesting to note the pupils' demands for somewhat incompatible or conflicting roles from teachers, and for the teacher to be able to judge the appropriateness of specific roles at specific times. For example:

"Kind but strict at the same time."

"Gotta be strict, willing to have a laugh at the same time."

Using Good Judgement

Teachers must use discipline that is appropriate.

Teachers must sensitively adopt different roles as necessary.

Further comments from pupils regarding 'good' teachers, and which further illustrate their expectations of such teachers include:

"Not lenient but knowing when to get angry."

"She knew when to stop being strict and when to stop being kind."

The pupils appear to have a strong sense of the various roles of the teacher. They expect these roles to rapidly and willingly change according to their needs. Clearly pupils with EBD place strong demands on teachers that are sometimes contradictory and involve a complex combination of humour, control and sensitivity. Such demands may be more significant for the pupil with EBD than mainstream pupils, reflecting the need for exceptional qualities and flexibility in teachers who are to be successful with such children.

One valuable quality that appeared to be particularly significant for some of the pupils was a sense of humour. Although discipline was important for the pupils it was most effective when combined with a 'human' side. Simon suggested that a good teacher is:

A Sense of Humour

A sense of humour is very valuable for teachers, especially with challenging pupils.

"Someone who can teach, but in a fun way. Have a laugh with them."

Such comments support previous work in the field such as Garner (1991) who states; 'A sense of humour seems to be a prerequisite for teaching "disruptive" students.' (p156). In fact according to research with mainstream pupils this appears to be an important attribute for teachers in any situation, not only pupils with EBD. (Times Educational Supplement, 1992).

In summary these comments appear to illustrate the fact that pupils can put quite difficult and uncompromising demands on teachers. As Cullingford (1991) suggests, there may be a tension between the personality of the individual teacher and the impersonal authority of the position, especially when dealing with large groups of children. Nevertheless their pupils demand that they deal with these difficulties if they are to be successful, particularly with more disturbing or difficult pupils.

Consistency and fairness

As an extension to discipline, the ability of a teacher to be consistent and fair was also important for the pupils interviewed. Mike, a 13 year old at Southdown School who had been bullied in the mainstream setting and had responded aggressively and with truancy, described a teacher who he perceived as having achieved consistency and fairness:

> "Helping the pupils in the class, not leaving them out. Not looking after some people and not the others. Looking after people equally, and making sure they each get the attention they need."

Consistency was also an important quality for Robert, who was quick to recall the inconsistency of one of his teachers with regards to homework. He described having been told off for not completing some homework but went on to say:

> "I remember a few months later other people hadn't done their homework and he just said do it tomorrow."

Similar perceptions were described by Sandra, who was a sensitive and often defensive 13 year old girl attending the Oakwood Centre. She was a school refuser who had experienced difficulties with the academic aspects of the secondary mainstream setting. She explained how she perceived her problems to be rooted in the teachers' unfairness and considered that she might have succeeded in mainstream if there had been more consistency with support:

> " If they'd paid more attention to me like they did everyone else."

She continued by saying:

> " I sat in the front row, but if I had my hand up she'd go to everyone else before she'd come to me."

It could be that the pupil with EBD has a heightened sense of injustice and responds rather quickly to any indication that they are being treated differently to others. Perhaps when already feeling insecure and different, they experience a more acute awareness of this issue than those pupils who are able to remain within the mainstream setting. For example Susan explained her feelings about teachers:

> "I don't trust teachers. They always blame me for everything."

Roy also commented on teachers and injustice with this comment:

> "Mrs. Smith irritated me, she believed everyone's story except mine."

This perceived lack of fairness by certain teachers is clearly an important aspect of how some pupils with EBD experience schooling and should be carefully explored in order to assess how it impacts on the behaviour of these pupils. Their perceptions may be seen as somewhat distorted or one-sided in the eyes of the professionals involved, yet it certainly exists as a major issue for these pupils. Some of the pupils clearly stated that they had wanted, needed and sought help from teachers in order to meet the demands of the classroom, yet felt they had been impeded by their teachers' unfair allocation of support. Less able pupils were particularly verbal in the inter-

Being Just and Consistent

Pupils with EBD show a heightened sensitivity to injustice and inconsistency.

43

views regarding their significant frustrations resulting from insufficient or inadequate support in lessons. This important issue for these pupils is of course closely related to the previous discussion concerning the effects of class size on the ability of the pupils to be educated within the mainstream setting. Johnny's perceptions of the difficulties he had faced were varied but he focused consistently on his anger at wanting to work and succeed yet not being given adequate help:

"You'd call her up and she'd not help you a bit."

Receiving inadequate support from teachers was also an important issue when security and feeling safe were in jeopardy, reflecting the social rather than academic aspects of the school and the needs of the pupils. Two pupils who were vulnerable to bullying and negative peer interaction commented on their frustration at teachers who they felt had offered inadequate support and had lacked true recognition of their difficulties:

Giving Adequate Support

Pupils with EBD are easily frustrated by a perceived lack of academic and social support.

"One teacher, who even knew it was going on, like in front of his face, didn't do anything about it…"

"They don't do anything, they just ignore it."

These pupils' social insecurities and related demands on teachers may reflect the highly individual and somewhat unique special needs of the child with EBD. Such needs appear to contrast with those of the succeeding mainstream pupil according to previous research in that setting. Larry, a 16 year old at the Oakwood Centre who had been unable to remain in mainstream because of his 'disruptive' behaviour, felt a keen sense of injustice at the way he had been treated by a specific teacher:

"I really hated her. If there was any fights or anything she'd come straight to me and my mate and half the time it wasn't us."

Being 'picked on' by one specific teacher was also a feeling experienced by Sandra who revealed a complex combination of reasons for her failure in mainstream schooling:

"She used to pick on me. She'd say I was skiving. She'd phone up my mum and tell her."

Sandra continued with a further criticism of teachers, that of colluding with other pupils:

Being Picked on

Some pupils with EBD feel they are being singled out by teachers.

"Like she used to tell my friends I was skiving … When they used to get to the classroom she'd say to them, right Sandra isn't here, she's skiving again today."

Similarly, Wayne perceived a teacher to have been colluding with his peer group. The following statement suggests that Wayne perceived the teacher to have encouraged discussion about him amongst his peers and may even have joined in with pupils who were discussing him in his absence:

44

"When I was away he'd actually take the Mickey out of me. He'd agree with everybody... and that didn't really help."

Cullingford (1993a) describes how experiences of injustice or unfairness, particularly that of being 'picked on', are very important experiences for pupils and remain 'seared in the mind.'(p59). Experiencing difficulty in a relationship with just one particular teacher appears to potentially create a negative and destructive situation for some pupils. Sandra described the complexity of the factors that had created her difficulties and along with her own personal weaknesses and the expectations of the curriculum also pinpointed one particular teacher.

"I think it was that teacher, the work, and 'cause I thought I was thick, and I didn't think I could do it."

A focus on one particular teacher reinforces the findings of Galloway et al (1982), who concluded from interviews with disruptive pupils that hostility was often focused on one member of staff and not on the school as a whole or on the teachers collectively. Galloway et al found that there were few pupils who were unable to discriminate between their attitudes to different teachers, with only 17% claiming to dislike all or most of the teachers in their schools. They discuss in some detail the role of negative teacher/pupil relationships in the development of particular pupils' difficulties in school, and they are actually able to quote that 32% of pupils in their study expressed an intense dislike or resentment of one particular individual teacher. They speculate that a long-standing personality clash between a pupil and a teacher could be at the root of some pupils' problems. These views are also in agreement with the work of Scherer et al (1990) who make similar observations from their enquiry with mainstream pupils. However, they suggest a more two directional flow of negative emotion, whereby an intense mutual dislike could at times be at the root of the child's problems at school. They propose that once such negative relationships have been established they become hard to break. Larry was particularly aware of his 'reputation' in the eyes of certain teachers, yet according to his perception of the situation he felt that his attempts to bring about change in his own behaviour and the bad relationships with these teachers were futile:

"We'd think we'd do our work today and we'd say where's our work and they'd say you won't do any anyway."

"We wouldn't do anything and they'd pick on us anyway."

This important issue, which may be referred to as labelling, will be discussed in more detail in the next chapter. At this point it is important that the reader be aware of the significant influence of relationships between specific teachers and pupils, including that teacher's fairness and consistency, in the evolution of pupil difficulties in school. In particular, pupils with EBD appear to require a high degree of fairness and justice in relationships with teachers. The descriptions of their own behaviour do however clearly illustrate how difficult this can be when they often demand attention from teachers in ways that may be considered inappropriate creating or perpetuating situations that the pupils themselves describe as being unacceptable!

Hostility between Pupils and Individual Teachers

A negative relationship with just one teacher can greatly impact the attitudes and behaviours of certain pupils.

Positive relationships

In contrast to the impact of negative relationships between teachers and pupils a number of the pupils in this study revealed the importance of positive relationships with one particular teacher or other adult in the school. Johnny talked of a close relationship with the headmaster of a primary school he had attended prior to being placed at the Oakwood Centre:

> "I wanted that headmaster to stay, so he could teach me all my life."

Unfortunately, although such a relationship can clearly be of great value to a pupil such as Johnny and possibly stabilise him within the mainstream setting, its loss can have devastating consequences, as he explained:

> "The headmaster used to come in and give me help with my work and my sums, and my English, my handwriting, my reading. He used to come in and see how I was doing and help me. He had to leave, and a new headmaster came in. I got thrown out a couple of days after he came in."

Johnny talked of many issues when asked about the possible reasons for his difficulties in school, including the breakdown of his parents' marriage and the departure of his mother from the home. In his particular case it is very tempting to suggest that the development of positive relationships with adults within the school were vitally important. This is further illustrated by his description of a relationship with the school secretary prior to his expulsion from mainstream:

> "I went to a secretary when I had troubles. She helped me out a lot, talked to me. I used to help her with jobs."

Gerry was another pupil who described how positive relationships with specific adults in the school had helped him to survive, albeit temporarily, in the mainstream setting:

> "Mrs. S she was most probably the best teacher there... She could understand about my things what I can't do. Gave me maths in the lesson that I could cope with then at break time do a little bit of reading everyday."

Gerry also described the value of a relationship with an adult in his school who was not a teacher similar to the support Johnny received from the secretary.

> "There was one teacher, she wasn't really a teacher... and she used to listen, we talked about a lot of things."

Jeremy, a 12 year old boy at Southdown School who had been expelled from mainstream school as a result of aggression towards peers, and other disruptive behaviours found some meaningful support from the school nurse:

"The school nurse, Joyce, she helped me."

It appears that a person in the school who was free from the role of teacher offered these pupils valuable help, of a non-academic nature. In some cases however that 'special' person could be a teacher, as illustrated by Wayne:

"I could always talk to Mr. X, he wouldn't shout and I could tell him everything."

These comments suggest that the essence of a successful supportive relationship in the school was one that involved an offer of time and the opportunity to talk on an individual basis. Interestingly only one pupil described useful support as coming from a member of staff who had been specifically employed as a school counsellor. Only Colin described how the counsellor at Southdown had played a significant role in enabling him to achieve some success in that setting

"Mr. W, he's one of my best friends. He's the school counsellor."

This member of staff appeared to offer what Colin perceived as friendship, and was not restricted to working with him within the confines of a teacher's role. This may be somewhat similar to the supporting role adopted by the secretary or school nurse as described by other pupils in the study. The fact that Colin was the only pupil in this present study who referred to a counsellor as providing him with any notable support, may of course simply reflect the lack of availability of such support within schools, rather than it being perceived as insignificant by the pupils being interviewed. The value of a counsellor within the mainstream school for pupils with the potential for EBD is illustrated in Cooper (1993b) in his account of one school's successful attempts to improve behaviour through curriculum development.

These descriptions of successful support give valuable insight into how pupils with EBD perceive their own needs, and how these needs may possibly contrast with those of mainstream pupils. The role of their teachers and other staff and the pupils' requirement of them are clearly complex. Interestingly it is the relationships between teachers and pupils that actually appear to be more important to some pupils with EBD, than the ability of the teacher to teach or discipline. Wanting their teachers to find time to build relationships and to know them better as individuals was particularly important to some pupils interviewed. Ten of them simply wanted teachers to listen to them, perceiving this basic interaction as contributing greatly to what makes a 'good' teacher. A small but significant number of pupils in the study felt that teachers didn't have the time to listen, didn't make the time to listen, or were unwilling to listen, resulting in misunderstandings. Being misunderstood was a frustration certainly expressed by Wayne when his response to being bullied and teased was to fight back. This resulted in himself being punished and he blamed this on a teacher:

"She wasn't willing to listen to your point of view."

He perceived that a good teacher would be:

Significant Relationships

Supportive individualised relationships with specific adults in the school can greatly benefit children with EBD.

"Talking to you, understanding you, asking why, giving you a chance to tell them."

He clearly stated his need for teachers to spend more time with him, and described one teacher whom he liked:

"She'd make time even if she didn't have time."

Gerry's description of a 'good' teacher was:

"She gets to know you, to know what you want."

"Well, listening and how she copes with you ... everybody's different."

From these comments it is tempting to suggest that pupils with EBD require somewhat closer relationships with teachers than mainstream pupils in order to support and help them with their intricate web of needs. However, succeeding mainstream pupils may have similar needs as Kutnick & Jules (1993) revealed when they investigated the perceptions of over a thousand 7 to 17 year old pupils in Trinidad and Tobago on 'a good teacher.' They sum up their findings with the following comment:

'...pupils desire a sensitive and supportive relationship with their teachers, a relationship that is not so much dominated by curriculum presentation as by a knowledge of and ability to work with the pupil.' (p412).

Teachers in Supportive Roles

Pupils want teachers to find the time to listen and get to know them as well as teach them.

Branwhite (1994) supports this view suggesting that schools must be prepared to continue to see themselves as caring agencies as well as institutions for academic learning, '...especially so in the current U.K. climate of schools being cast by the government largely as a delivery system for the National Curriculum.' (p67). In his 1988 study he investigated the qualities of teachers valued by five hundred and ninety five, 13 to 16 year olds and empathy was considered very important, characterised by amongst other things, being friendly, listening, staying calm. This suggests that all pupils, not only pupils with EBD do place importance on the teacher as a carer. In fact Branwhite highlights an interesting observation made by Galbo (1989) that the characteristics and qualities that adolescents desire in their relationships with teachers are those that adults prefer with each other. This relates to Kutnick & Jules (1993) who refer to pupils desiring a mutual respect between the teacher and the pupil.

Simon, at Southdown, was an articulate, intelligent boy, who summed up his ideas regarding relationships with teachers:

" Treat us like normal people, not like some little school kids."

Miller (1994) throws interesting light on the way disruptive pupils perceive the teacher/pupil relationship. In her research with bright disruptive pupils in the mainstream setting, the pupils explained their disruptions as '...a rational response to the inappropriateness of the curriculum and the lack of attention and consideration they received as persons.' (p252). These pupils felt that they had not been given the opportunity to be known as real people within the school setting. The research suggests that these pupils have quite different needs to slow learners who display behaviour problems. The bright pupils in her study were dissatisfied with the limited role of the teacher who concentrates totally on getting through the work, limiting their communication and interactions with the pupils to interactions about work, commands or threats. They also perceived their own mindless and subordinate role as being forced onto them by the school. In keeping with the views of other school pupils, including those at the Oakwood Centre and Southdown, these pupils were also particularly sensitive to injustice and hypocrisy.

The pupils' plea for a chance to lose their subordinate pupil role and develop a more intense, perhaps collegial role with teachers was certainly echoed by a few of the brighter pupils in the present study. Some felt that the special school setting had allowed them to develop closer and more productive relationships with teachers including Karen who was very positive about the teachers at the Oakwood Centre:

Respect

Pupils want relationships with teachers based on mutual respect.

> "They talk and care a lot, they understand."

The use of first names is often another interesting indication of the type of relationship that exists between teachers and their pupils and significantly this is often one of the major differences between the mainstream and the special school setting for pupils with EBD. It was raised by 15 year old Dave who stated that one of the differences he perceived between Southdown School and the mainstream schools from which he had been expelled, particularly in terms of his improved relationships with teachers, was:

> "Being allowed to call teachers by their first names."

Perhaps such apparently simple issues can mean more to certain pupils than we as professionals are aware.

Meeting the individual's needs

Some of the pupils with EBD judged a teacher to be 'good' or 'bad' based on whether that teacher was able to meet their own very specific individual personal needs and demands in the classroom. The pupils' needs were often focused on making progress with classroom work, being given praise, or simply getting by, surviving without failure or humiliation. Such survival did not necessarily equate with learning. Analysis of the comments made by the pupils illustrates the importance of understanding the very unique perceptions of survival in the classroom that may be held by pupils with EBD. For example Sandra, who was very clear about the traits of a good teacher, gave a good example of this:

> "Good teachers are ones that let you chat to your friends in class about work."

She admitted to being unable to keep up with a lot of the class work and being frightened of getting into trouble as a result:

"I was so scared cause everyone else could but I was the only one who couldn't."

Sandra perceived that she had not experienced major problems in school prior to her transition to the secondary setting. At the primary level she appeared to have successfully used her friends to support her and possibly help her disguise her academic weaknesses:

"I had loads of people sit next to me and help me. I'm relying on my friends more than anything."

The secondary school however had placed increased demands on her in terms of the curriculum, and removed the peer support structures that had nurtured and assisted her through earlier schooling. This loss appeared to have created an unmanageable and somewhat intimidating situation for her.

Measor & Woods (1984) consider the transfer to secondary school to be a difficult time for pupils who have relied on informal peer support within the classroom. They state that; 'The change of school seemed to threaten this informal - but to pupils essential - activity for handling formal requirements.' (p15). The secondary classroom requirements appear to allow fewer of the informal survival strategies that pupils such as Sandra have developed to disguise weaknesses. For Sandra removal of this support resulted in the development of negative relationships with teachers. Those who denied her the survival strategies that she so relied on exposed her weaknesses and appeared to threaten her self-esteem. Her happiness in the classroom and her assessment of teachers depended strongly on whether talking was allowed in class and whether pupils were allowed to interact. Her comments suggest that the goal of certain pupils with EBD in schools may be to simply maintain an emotional 'peace' and to survive with the minimum of embarrassment. Their concern with academic achievement or progress may be secondary to these concerns.

George, an insecure boy, of quite low ability, also felt more secure when he was able to use his peers for support in the classroom and it was his perception that a good teacher did not deny him his survival strategies. Only if he was allowed to talk to his friends did he feel that he could do the class work and learn. He described one teacher whom he liked:

"He wanted you to do the work, but he didn't mind how you did it... like you could talk and work at the same time ... If the teacher tells you to be quiet, you don't get the hang of it."

It is obviously difficult for teachers to assess the amount of learning that takes place when pupils work together, but the statements made by these pupils appear to support some of the suggestions of Measor & Woods (1984), who propose the term 'co-operation groups' (p14) to describe the way pupils use peer groups to support themselves through the formal demands of the classroom. They describe these groups as being based on friendship ties and containing a hierarchy that determines the roles of different pupils. Measor & Woods state that of the pupils on which they based their research '...most found at least some consultation with their fellows indispensable to their

Trying to Survive

Pupils want teachers to recognise their own perceived needs.

Pupils needs are often linked to surviving without embarrassment or failure.

Removing Support

Teachers who remove informal support structures in the classroom may be perceived negatively by pupils.

50

learning'. (p15). When needed, questions such as 'Do you know?', 'I'm stuck', or 'Start me off' are considered by Measor & Woods to be acceptable pleas for help. Barrett (1984) also recognises the importance of peer support in certain situations; 'The freedom to use self help and that of other people without being accused of cheating or copying appear to create a powerful learning strategy.' (p36). However, it would seem that for some pupils with EBD in this present study, learning was not as much their concern as simply surviving. For them, using peers for support in the classroom may be for the purpose of survival and the avoidance of humiliation rather than any concern with academic achievement. This was the case for Sandra:

> "They used to assume because I was copying off my mates, that I could do the work."

When she was denied this back up or survival strategy, Sandra did not have the courage to reveal her true weaknesses, and stopped attending:

> "Cause I knew I couldn't keep up with the work. I didn't wanna get into trouble."

The potential humiliation or other perceived consequences resulting from being unable to do the work were powerful enough to result in attendance problems for this pupil. Humiliation appeared to result from what peers would think or being told off by the teacher. Roy was a school refuser who described feeling vulnerable with certain teachers who would tell him off for making mistakes or not being able to do the work. He described one teacher who:

> "Would have a go at kids for doing things wrong."

When given some English work that he found too hard, he was afraid that the teacher would:

> "Have a go at him."

An understanding of the pupils' motives for seeking peer support is obviously of great importance within mainstream schools if teachers are to successfully work with pupils with EBD and teachers may need to find ways to allow peer support yet also guarantee learning. This is difficult, as there appear to be other less desirable motives for being allowed to talk in class, as Keys & Fernandes (1993) discovered in their research with succeeding mainstream pupils. These pupils stated that they liked to work with friends because they found schoolwork boring. Similarly Quicke (1994) refers to the work of Marsh, Rosser & Harre (1978), who found that pupils wanted to chatter and have a bit of fun, reinforcing evidence that certain pupils do not only seek peer interaction for the sake of learning or academic survival.

Returning to a pupil's definition or description of a 'good' or 'bad' teacher, interviews with Johnny revealed that certain pupils desired a person who promptly met their own individual needs. Johnny clearly needed close and constant support in the classroom:

Ensuring Learning Through Peer Support

Teachers must find ways to provide support structures that allow learning to take place.

51

"A good teacher is one who comes to me first."

Roy was also able to verbalise his specific needs regarding teachers:

"Sets you work that is do-able and who compliments me."

One of the problems for pupils with EBD is that in a mainstream classroom meeting these demands may not be practical or acceptable. For example Jeremy at Southdown was a pupil who readily exploded with anger when confronted with certain situations. His perception of a good teacher was one who:

"Lets you walk out."

Special Needs

The highly individualised needs of certain pupils with EBD may be difficult to meet in a mainstream setting and require a high degree of flexibility.

Although difficult to allow in a mainstream setting, such individual perception could be valuable when attempting to support this particular pupil in school. Such perceptions reflect the highly diverse and individual needs of the child with EBD who needs a somewhat different approach from those pupils who are able to remain in the mainstream setting.

Thus, teachers have the difficult job of trying to unravel the true motives and needs behind pupils' behaviours. Confusion over motives may not help pupils with EBD in mainstream classrooms, as teachers may not always respond appropriately to challenging behaviours. Certain behaviours may in fact be meeting the needs of their pupils and therefore cannot simply be eliminated.

Key points emerging from this section

- Increasing research has focussed on how pupils with EBD perceive their teachers.

- Some pupils with EBD perceive their teachers as contributing to the difficulties they experience in a mainstream setting.

- Teachers who are successful with challenging pupils appear to possess particular skills and personality traits.

- Some pupils criticise teachers for not finding the time to communicate with them and build relationships.

Thoughts for your reflection

- Consider your own strengths and weaknesses as a teacher based on the pupils' perceptions presented in this section.

- Do you adequately consider the emotional needs of a child when planning instruction or managing behaviour?

- Are your discipline techniques truly effective in supporting acceptable behaviour and changing misbehaviour?

Tips for improving your success with difficult or challenging children

- Constantly develop the necessary classroom and behaviour management skills in order to feel that you are in control of your own classroom at all times.

- Do not shout at pupils when disciplining.

- Retain control of your own emotions.

- Take particular care if you ever touch a pupil when disciplining them.

- Try to ensure that pupils feel that the 'punishment' fits the crime.

- Use careful judgement in deciding which role you should adopt with challenging pupils at different times.

- Have a sense of humour.

- Be consistent and aware of being fair at all times.

- Be aware of how much emotional and academic support certain pupils need.

- Be careful not to be perceived as singling out certain pupils unnecessarily.

- Be prepared for hostility from certain pupils.

- Take every opportunity to build positive relationships with pupils based on mutual respect whenever possible.

- Don't just teach, take the time to talk and listen to pupils.

- Try to be sensitive to the needs of your pupils and the informal peer supports they may be relying on in your classroom to survive.

- Develop the flexibility that is necessary for a successful approach to children with EBD.

3.1 (iii) **The curriculum**

A number of the pupils made interesting statements about the way in which the curriculum had contributed to their behavioural difficulties. In many cases these curriculum issues appeared to be closely linked to other factors such as teachers, class size and peer interaction.

The curriculum and teachers

The statements made by the pupils that focused on the curriculum were often either subject specific, teacher specific or a combination of both. Some statements suggested a somewhat confusing relationship between the teachers' skills and personalities and the curriculum content being presented. This point is clearly illustrated by two pupils who stated:

> " I used to hate most of the lessons because of the teachers."

> " If I don't like the teachers I don't do the work."

Unpopular Teachers

Certain subjects are disliked because of the teacher teaching it.

It would appear that not liking a teacher or teachers could be closely related to not liking or co-operating with the demands of the curriculum in that class. The extent to which the opposite may be true was not clear from the results of this study although some subject areas were perceived for a variety of reasons to be more unpopular than others. It was also not clear to what extent a teacher's personality and professional skills could overcome the constraints of being associated with an unpopular subject area, but it would seem that some teachers could be somewhat disadvantaged in terms of pupil approval by the subject that they teach.

Unpopular curriculum areas

The pupils revealed certain subjects to be particularly unpopular and in some cases influential in establishing behaviour patterns such as truancy. Other subjects simply appeared to enhance feelings of vulnerability for certain pupils and these feelings manifested themselves in a variety of disturbing or unacceptable behaviours. One particularly unpopular subject was physical education (PE) which was described previously as a problem when discussing class sizes. Seven of the pupils interviewed commented on feelings of humiliation and inadequacy during PE both in the eyes of their peers and teachers. Robert stated that not wanting to do PE would be one major problem that would interfere with his attempt at reintegrating back into mainstream. For Karen, a large, shy girl whose body image was negative and who had been bullied, PE appeared to have offered plenty of opportunity for victimisation and embarrassment:

> "When it started to get to cross country, imagine me running round a field, people taking the Mickey out of you for your size and stuff. You have to wear those little shorts. If you slacked they made you do twice as much. Trampolining was the worst, everyone laughing, looking underneath saying 'do you know how far it went down when you jumped?'. Spiteful things."

Other pupils described behaviours that had allowed them to avoid this subject:

> "At Middle School, always ill on games days."

> "Sometimes when I had PE I used to deliberately hide my kit, so I wouldn't do it. I hate it."

Julie was another shy girl who mentioned PE as having been a problem for her in the mainstream school. She stated that she, " hated it", and went on to explain the humiliation of having to strip off in front of people to take a shower. Roy was another pupil commenting negatively about this subject:

"In PE, I wasn't sporty, I got tired quickly and the teachers, I didn't get on with."

Wayne similarly linked his lack of ability to his dislike of this subject:

"And PE, I never liked it, no good at it."

Clearly these statements illustrate the kinds of problems that a pupil may experience if forced to participate in a class in which he or she feels threatened or inadequate. These feelings are consistent with the findings of O'Keeffe & Stoll (1995) whose investigation into truancy and school attendance problems within the mainstream setting found PE to be a lesson from which many of the pupils truanted.

Being aware of pupils' motives for problem behaviours that are in any way linked to the curriculum is obviously important when devising ways to maintain them in the mainstream setting. Reasons given by mainstream pupils for their disaffection are often related to the subject being boring or irrelevant, too difficult, providing too much coursework or homework that they could not keep up with, or was taught by a teacher they did not get on with. Certainly the pupils with EBD in this present study, such as Karen, agreed with these reasons yet also described the impact of humiliation and embarrassment in certain subject areas that had led to avoidance behaviours. For pupils with EBD it is possible that PE exacerbates other emotional problems or difficulties that the pupil is experiencing, such as bullying which may or may not be significant to mainstream pupils.

In addition to PE, foreign languages were also described as being unpopular or a problem by several pupils in this study. Disillusioned with his experiences in mainstream school, Larry explained why he felt that studying French was irrelevant:

"They should give you lessons that help you about what you wanna be instead of chucking French and the rest of that crap at ya."

He added later in the interview:

"I don't see the point of learning a different language if you're never gonna go to that country."

Roy illustrated how a subject such as French can become disliked and unpopular simply because a pupil is not good at it:

" I was alright in some lessons, but French really mucked me up. I don't think the teacher liked me... I used to be hopeless at it."

His statement also suggests that pupils perceive teachers as only liking those who are good at their subject, an issue that must be addressed by teachers working to encourage the success of all pupils in their classrooms. This is consistent with the pupils who specifically disliked PE because they considered themselves inadequate at it.

Physical Education

PE appears to be a particularly unpopular subject for certain children.

Fear of humiliation can lead to attempts at avoiding it.

Avoiding Unpopular Subjects

Certain unpopular subjects may be linked to behaviours such as truancy.

Certain subjects may exacerbate other emotional or social problems for children with EBD.

One pupil had a negative perception of geography:

"I don't see the point of it."

Another perceived religious education as irrelevant:

"If you don't believe in God then you shouldn't do it."

If an irrelevant or boring curriculum is one of the major reasons given by mainstream pupils for truancy or other problems (O'Keeffe and Stoll, 1995, Pasternicki et al, 1993) then clearly schools and policy makers must focus on providing a curriculum that is perceived by all pupils as relevant to their needs. This may be a key area to address if those pupils currently labelled as EBD and disaffected with mainstream schooling are to remain in that setting. In order for this to happen however it is clearly important to attempt to better understand the underlying origin of each pupil's problems with the curriculum, as this may differ for each individual.

Low ability pupils and the curriculum

Some researchers have attempted to analyse exactly why pupils become bored or find work irrelevant. Scherer et al (1990) have focused on those of less ability and propose that the pupils 'may regard striving for the meagre certificates they are likely to obtain as simply not worthwhile.' (p15). O'Keeffe & Stoll (1995) describe how the negative feelings relating to certain subjects described by the pupils in their study were simply a result of the subject being perceived as too difficult, which is consistent with a number of statements made by pupils with EBD in the present study. Some of the pupils who found the work too difficult were clearly able to justify their behaviours as being a result of these academic difficulties, thus suggesting a significant link between the curriculum and disturbing behaviours. Norwich (1994) cites Hart (1992) who states that '...learning difficulties arise when there is a mismatch between the curriculum that is provided and the abilities, interests and optimum learning styles of individual pupils.' (p291). In support of this statement, Gerry stated:

"I would just sit there and not do it cause I wouldn't be able to unless it was easy...unless I could read it."

He described various strategies that he had used when faced with work that was too difficult for him, including the following:

"I used to make up excuses, dropping my ruler and stuff like that. I've lost my pencil, I need a rubber, to get out of it, to stop being embarrassed."

He also added:

"I only used to say I'm not doing it or walk out."

He appeared to be adopting actions that helped avoid embarrassment or humiliation and possibly enabled him to maintain a certain degree of personal control over the situation. To state "I'm not going to do it" may be preferable to "I can't do it" for many pupils. The two statements are significantly different in terms of how a student like Gerry might be perceived by his peer group. It appears that facing formal punishment such as detention was preferable to admitting that the work was too difficult or trying and failing:

"I would just sit there, they'd give me a detention after school."

Danny also preferred to choose unacceptable behaviour and the consequences of such behaviour, as opposed to having to do the work that he was being given:

"I mucked about so I could get sent out of class so I wouldn't have to do the work."

In certain cases pupils were simply resigned to the fact that the work was too hard for them and they did not blame the school:

"It was a good school, but the work was too hard."

A few pupils were willing to blame themselves for their problems with the curriculum and recognised that they had difficulties keeping up with classroom expectations:

"In work I was behind all the time."

Julie perceived a direct link between her difficulties with the curriculum and the behaviours that finally resulted in her being labelled as a student with EBD in a special school:

"I have trouble with reading. I was taken out of my English lesson for special help with my reading. But when I went to the next English lesson where they were reading big books, I fell so far behind with it because I also had to take it home and read it, and I never bothered to read it. Then I had to do all about it, and do loads of homework. I couldn't do it. I fell behind on all my work so I stopped going to school."

Many of the pupils' comments illustrate how demoralised they had become within the mainstream setting, and how resigned they were to accepting their difficulties. Sandra and Ken made the following statements respectively:

"I was just thick."

"The teachers are just doing their job and if I don't understand that's my fault."

Sadly, these pupils located the blame for their schooling difficulties solely within themselves and regretted their behaviours:

"I took the easy way out. If I'd tried it I could still be there."

Avoiding Difficult Work.

Some low functioning pupils adopt behavioural strategies that enable them to avoid difficult work or school itself.

Low Self Esteem

Certain pupils perceive themselves as inadequate.

The curriculum and able pupils

Two pupils in the study encouraged a closer look at the impact of the curriculum on the behavior of particularly able pupils. The behaviour of the bright but disruptive pupils interviewed in a study by Miller (1994) is described as being a result of '...a frustration with the inappropriateness of academic expectations...' or '...an attempt to compensate for being unpopular with peers because of academic success.' (p252). The following statement made by Ronnie, a bright 16 year old delinquent attending Southdown as a result of drug abuse and truancy, suggests that able pupils can make their own decisions regarding whether or not to conform to curriculum demands:

> "I always knew I could do it, I just didn't wanna."

Being Different

Bright pupils may avoid displaying their intelligence.

Karen did not enjoy the fact that being more academically able than others had made her feel different and lonely:

> "The teacher would ask a question and I'd always be the one to put my hand up or answer the question and people would say 'boffin' and all that."

Her mother had tried to keep her in line with other pupils despite being more academically able than them:

> "She thought she might as well keep me in that year rather than take me out, and then finishing before everyone, and being even more out of it, even more different."

This point illustrates how able pupils may need particular sensitivity in the classroom when they attempt to meet curriculum demands. Teachers must be aware of how the curriculum and its mode of presentation particularly within the mainstream school can exacerbate feelings of being different for certain pupils with EBD.

Homework

For pupils already struggling with work in the classroom, homework for some appeared to be another opportunity for conflict with the school or teachers. Seven pupils raised the issue of homework as contributing to their difficulties:

> "A teacher had a go at me cause I hadn't done my homework, but I didn't understand it."

> "I got really worried about the homework."

> "I found homework difficult."

> "I just couldn't do the homework. I just couldn't remember what I was being taught."

> "I got really worried about the homework in French."

"The work was really hard, loads of homework."

As these comments reveal, difficulties with academic work were often compounded by homework expectations and created anxiety in certain pupils. Little research appears to have specifically focused on this issue from the perspective of the pupil with EBD, although these results do show some similarities to those of O'Keeffe & Stoll (1995). Their study of pupils in mainstream schools suggested that truancy could be related to schools providing too much coursework or homework and that the pupils felt unable to keep up with the demands. George explained how his frequent absence from school as a result of bullying led to additional problems related to homework when he did attend:

"I never used to do it, cause then I used to find it hard. I never used to go, homework used to be like the lesson I'd missed, so I never used to know what we was doing and no-one used to tell me."

His statement illustrates how it may become increasingly difficult for a pupil to reintegrate back into a mainstream school once a pattern of non-attendance has been established, owing to difficulties resulting from missing classes and being unable to understand and complete homework. He explained how difficulties in returning to school were increased as a result of the school's punishments for incomplete homework:

"If you didn't do homework you'd get debits and detentions."

Sandra described how supportive parents may alleviate homework difficulties although that did not help her academic problems in the classroom:

"It was alright if it was homework because I could ask my Mum to help me, but if it was like in the school, I'm relying on my friends more than anything."

For Wayne simply having to take work home was just too much:

"The homework just reminded me of school, so I thought, I'm not going to do it."

Epstein, Polloway & Foley (1993) present evidence that pupils with behavioural disorders or learning disabilities are perceived by teachers and parents as having more significant homework problems. If this is the case then teachers must be fully aware of the nature of the pupils' difficulties, especially when supporting them in the mainstream setting.

Involving pupils in curriculum issues

The involvement of pupils themselves in the development of an appropriate curriculum is recognised in official documentation on curriculum issues. Garner (1993b) quotes The National Curriculum Council's document 'A Curriculum for All' (1989), as stating that students have a strong need for 'partnerships with teachers which encourage them to become active learners, helping

Keeping up with Demands

Many pupils find the demands of homework too great.

Difficulty attending school can be exacerbated by homework expectations.

them to plan, build and evaluate their own learning programmes wherever possible.' (p405). However, despite this advice and research reinforcing it, such democracy can remain absent particularly in a mainstream setting. Some pupils in the present study made interesting comparisons between their special school provision and mainstream schools in terms of the degree of control over their own education they felt they had been given. Simon explained how he felt that his special school setting should and did differ from the mainstream school:

> "This is a special school, so we should do special things, and have choices."

Partnerships and Active Learners

Certain pupils perceive the special school setting as offering them more control over their own learning.

Two pupils at the Oakwood Centre stated the importance of giving pupils more choice and providing them with greater responsibility for their own work. They commented positively about their special provision:

> "You have choices. Choose what you wanna do."

> "You got to do your work and be responsible for yourself here."

Disaffection and the Curriculum

A curriculum perceived as meaningful and valid may reduce disaffection and problem behaviours.

A number of researchers have stated the importance of involving pupils in curriculum planning and encouraging co-operation between staff and pupils including Cooper (1993b), and Garner (1993b). Garner stresses that schools should have a vested interest in a curriculum that their consumers consider meaningful and rewarding. He states that it has been argued that pupils' exclusions are often for a serious misdemeanor '...which represents the final stages of a continuum that has originated in their dissatisfaction with the curriculum.' (p404). Schostak (1983) agrees that pupils themselves should be given a voice regarding the work that they do in schools, describing this as a self-elected curriculum. However, the difficulties associated with teaching large classes and setting differentiated material for highly individual needs within a dictated curriculum should not be underestimated and a realistic answer to these problems may be difficult to find.

Key points emerging from this section

- A successful curriculum for children with EBD needs to consider their wide-ranging social, emotional and behavioural needs.

- A compulsory curriculum for schools may seek equality but can reduce recognition of individual needs.

- Mainstream schools face the challenge of meeting the demands of a National Curriculum and also supporting the individualised needs of pupils with EBD.

Thoughts for your reflection

- Do you try to ensure the relevancy of the curriculum in your classroom to all children?

- Are you sensitive to the feelings of children who are easily humiliated or embarrassed?

- Do you involve pupils wherever possible in discussing curriculum content?

- Are you aware of the difficulties your homework expectations may create for certain pupils?

- Are you aware of how low levels of self-esteem may influence a child's behaviour in your classroom?

Tips for improving your success with difficult or challenging children

- Be careful to ensure that children are never made to feel inadequate or are humiliated in your classroom.

- Be aware that children with EBD may have a complexity of issues and the challenges in your classroom may be adding further stress.

- Try to make the curriculum content of your classroom relevant to the lives and values of your pupils.

- Be aware of pupils who can use certain behaviours to avoid work or school.

- Be aware that bright pupils may experience negative peer comments and pressure to underachieve.

- Don't let homework create further problems for pupils who are already struggling to attend or keep up.

- Try to give pupils a sense of control over how and what they learn.

3.1 (iv) **Social problems**

A significant number of the pupils in the study were articulate in expressing views regarding the role of the social aspects of schools in the creation and evolution of their difficulties and their subsequent placement in special education. In addition to those school factors previously described such as the curriculum, school and class size, the nature of school buildings and the attitudes and skills of teachers, a number of pupils also demonstrated a high level of comprehension and awareness of the social world of the school and its significance as a problem for them. They offered valuable insight into factors within their mainstream schools that may have nurtured such problems and their descriptions of their own behaviour and the motives for that behaviour were frequently associated with experiences of negative social interaction with peers.

The term they most frequently used was bullying. This section uses pupil statements to clarify the nature and extent of such behaviour and to assess the reasons why it appears to play such a critical role in the failure of many pupils with EBD to succeed in mainstream schools.

The Social World of the School

Social factors may nurture problems for children with EBD in mainstream schools.

The nature of bullying

Despite our growing familiarity with the word bullying its definition can be somewhat vague and it is hoped that the pupils' perceptions will help to clarify the exact nature of this type of behaviour. A number of the pupils were able to offer interesting descriptions of behaviours that they themselves classified as bullying. Some had been responsible for initiating these behaviours, whilst others had been victims. They described a range of activities and incidents that had occurred in both mainstream and special education settings including stealing and the destruction of personal possessions. Gerry told of bullying that occurred at a residential school prior to his arrival at the Oakwood Centre:

> "... people used to come in and break my Walkman, take my stuff and that used to annoy me."

Karen explained her experiences in mainstream school:

> "They used to nick your bag, pens and your coat, and throw your stuff on the floor."

Roy also experienced bullying in the form of stealing in his mainstream school:

> "Money going missing, shoes and clothes."

George described bullying as a behaviour he had adopted:

> "Give us your money or sweets or we'll beat you up."

Yet he also described his own victimisation:

> "Name calling and stuff like that, nicking books."

Physical abuse was described by six pupils in the study, but this did not include numerous accounts of fighting which are described in more detail in chapter 4. Karen described two different aggressive incidents that she had experienced in the mainstream school:

> "There were loads of them, they grabbed me from behind and she stuck all her nails in and started punching my face."

> "They would sit behind you and stick compasses in you."

Wayne and Roy also described physical aggression that they had experienced:

> "I was walking down the corridor and people grabbed me, rammed me up against the wall, and this person was hitting me."

> "A boy called Rick who found it amusing to hit me in the stomach."

Roy went on to explain other incidents:

> "Even the little kids, spitting and swearing at me on the way home ...gobbed on my back."

> "I was being hit, pushed, called names, hung up by my bag over a post and pinned up against a wall."

Bobby, a 15 year old boy at Southdown who had an aggressive history of bullying and delinquency, described his experiences of being a victim:

> "I was up against the wall, 'You're gonna die at lunchtime'."

Another boy at Southdown School, 12 year old Michael who had been living in care for most of his life and who had shown particularly extreme emotional and behavioural difficulties within the mainstream setting, reported how he had seen friends bullied:

> "They push my friends down the drive. They push them over."

Mike described his play-time experiences with peers:

> "At play time they used to come over and kick me and push me under the huts. They used to push you and keep you under there and it wasn't very nice."

Experiences Of Bullying

Bullying encompasses a variety of actions and events that have created problems for pupils.

Interestingly these aggressive, threatening behaviours were not always restricted to the school environment. Three pupils described bullying as extending beyond the school itself. Wayne recalled a trip to a fairground during which he perceived his vulnerability to be greater than in school:

> "They said go away boring and smashed my head against the Waltzer."

George recalled an incident where an abusive letter was put through his letterbox at home:

> "After school, one of the kids who lived across the road, wrote a letter and he stuffed it through the letter box and ran down the road."

Out of School Bullying

Bullying does not occur only in school.

Karen tried to attend a youth club but found problems with bullying to be present there. She said:

> "I stopped going to youth club because of it. I took my bike and someone let the tyres down."

These pupils seemed to be aware that they could be more vulnerable out of school than within. George and Karen continued respectively by stating:

> "If you can stop it at school, you can't really stop it at home."

"At youth club it was easier for them there, no teachers."

Perceptions of Bullying

Pupils give consistent descriptions of bullying.

Adults may not observe all incidents of bullying and may have different perceptions from those of the pupils.

The descriptions of actions of a threatening or physical nature given by the pupils in this study were similar to the results of other studies. For example Arora (1994) lists unpleasant actions described by mainstream pupils as 'tried to kick me, threatened to hurt me, demanded money from me, tried to hurt me, tried to hit me, tried to break something that belonged to me.' (p157). The consistency in results from various research projects which have used pupils' perceptions to determine what constitutes an act of bullying show that the pupils themselves appear to have little problem describing and defining bullying. However, these perceptions may differ somewhat from those of adults or professionals and as a result of the fact that many actions are not observed directly by anyone other than the pupils themselves.

The pupils' comments are also in close agreement with previous research revealing that verbal threats or mental bullying had often played as large a part in the pupils' difficulties and unhappiness as actual physical aggression. (Sharp, 1995). Wayne explained how destructive such behaviour had been to him:

> "Mental bullying is awful. Physical bullying OK, you can take it, a few bruises OK, naffed up leg, a few black eyes, OK you can take that. But when it's mental and it's not about me, about my parents and my family, it's just I can't take that."

Another form of bullying that fits into the category of subtle, emotional abuse is social exclusion. Karen described this type of bullying as particularly disturbing to her:

> "She'd make excuses like, 'there's not enough room at the table'."

> "They say 'why don't you just get out, we don't want you here'."

Perhaps it is the shrewd and indirect nature of this type of action that makes it so unpleasant and often undetectable by teachers or adults. It appears to attack the individual's sense of self worth and Siann, Callaghan, Glissov, Lockhart & Rawson (1994) describe this with clarity when they state; 'The subjective experience of feeling bullied relates... to being made to feel personally inferior and inadequate - it is a powerful assault on one's level of self esteem.' (p132). They also make the point that verbal bullying may involve comments that '...strike at the individual's private core of self...' (p133). Karen recalled her experience of such wounding comments:

Types of Bullying

Bullying may involve both physical and mental abuse.

> "Someone comes up to you and says, 'what is the meaning of your life, why don't you just die?' "

For certain pupils such as Karen, there was such a fear of bullying and its intentions, that she became distressed even when it was not actually happening. She explained her feeling:

> "Even when I wasn't, it was the fear of getting bullied."

Galloway (1994) believes that some schools have less bullying than others due to the successful creation of a climate that is 'relatively free from the fear of bullying.' (p25). Clearly there is the potential for an undercurrent of fear to develop in schools and this is something that they should be aware of despite the difficulties detecting or dealing with it. Measor & Woods (1984) interviewed pupils who were moving from middle to secondary school and found that at this point of transition their main worries were losing one's friends and '...the prospect of being bullied.' (p9). Francis & Jones (1994) quote research that states that even the word bullying itself evokes fear in many pupils and they propose a common thread running through the many definitions of bullying by stating; 'The fundamental attitude underlying victimization is that of fear.' (p113). Larry supports this proposal when describing his anxiety about another peer:

> "I used to be really scared of him."

It is certainly important that adults do not perceive the fears of certain children as irrational. Whitney, Nabuzoka & Smith (1992) quote the Headteacher of a centre for young people with 'school phobia' as saying that '...although a phobia such as school phobia is classified as an irrational fear, there are many aspects of schooling where a fear reaction is not at all an irrational response....' (p4). Francis & Jones (1994) describe some of the behaviours and emotions resulting from this fear, such as poor attitudes to school, fear of coming to school and truancy. They also describe extreme cases where the fear of bullying leads to physical injury, attempted suicide and even successful suicide.

The prevalence of bullying

A large number of pupils described experiencing negative social peer interaction in their mainstream schools. In total twenty -eight pupils described social problems as an experience that had contributed to their school difficulties although thirty-three pupils were able to comment about bullying having experienced or observed it, without necessarily stating its importance to them personally. In addition to making specific comments regarding their own experiences, certain pupils showed a more general awareness of the extensiveness of bullying within their schools. Simon and Bobby were both boys who appeared resigned to the fact that bullying was an intrinsic part of schooling:

> "Bullying is a way of life."

> "If they expelled everybody who did something cruel, the school would have one pupil or a few people in it."

This type of comment is not exclusive to pupils with EBD. Arnold (1994) reports pupils and teachers in a middle school using words and expressions such as 'normal' and 'getting used to it,' (p184), when describing bullying. Cullingford (1993a) suggests that perhaps bullying can be ignored because it merges so 'inextricably' with the whole experience of schooling. (p54). He states it is '...the way that bullying blends into the everyday life of the school, that makes it so worrying.' (p54). If an act of bullying can take on so many different forms and can so easily disguise itself as acceptable 'normal' behav-

The Role of Schools

It is possible for schools to take actions to reduce bullying and fear.

Real Fear

Fear of bullying in school or phobic reactions to school should not be considered irrational.

Who gets Bullied?

Very large numbers of pupils appear to be affected by bullying.

iour within schools, then clearly this explains why statistical reporting of bullying incidents in schools may create problems and be inconsistent. Robinson and Maines (1997) describe recent research into the prevalence of bullying in schools but they also acknowledge that data collection can be difficult and based on memory or subjective accounts.

Bullying and Pupils with EBD

Pupils with EBD may be more involved in bullying than other pupils.

Bullying may contribute significantly to the failure of pupils with EBD in mainstream schools.

Pervin & Turner (1994) report the results of a study carried out by Sheffield University in twenty four Sheffield Schools in the early 1990's, which revealed 27% of pupils in junior/middle schools reported having been bullied occasionally, and 10% being bullied once or more than once per week. In the secondary schools, 10% of pupils reported being bullied occasionally and 4% being bullied once or more per week. Pervin & Turner (1994) do however dispute these somewhat low figures, claiming that in their own study of one hundred and forty seven year 8 pupils, 50% of the boys and one-third of the girls claimed to have been bullied. In fact there is now even more recent evidence for numbers being higher than those quoted by Pervin & Turner. (Daily Telegraph, 1997). It is interesting to compare these figures from mainstream school studies with those from the present study in which 78% of the pupils raised social interaction with peers as one of the factors contributing to their difficulties in schools. This appears to reflect a greater incidence of bullying for pupils with EBD and emphasises how critical it is for teachers and other professionals to understand the role and significance of negative social experiences in the failure of pupils with EBD in mainstream schools. One way of developing such understanding is to explore the factors that enhance the risk of a child being a victim or bully.

Who are the bullies and victims?

Given the apparently high level of involvement of pupils with EBD in bullying incidents in schools, there is clearly a need to explore the characteristics of children that may enhance their risk of being a bully or a victim in order to offer them more support. Some of the pupils in this present study offered valuable insight into these characteristics and also showed a high degree of understanding of the underlying motives behind certain behaviours.

One of the factors related closely to victimisation and bullying which has been described by a number of researchers in this field (Measor & Woods, 1984, Cullingford, 1991, Olweus, 1994) and is supported by the pupils with EBD in the present study, was that of a pupil's group membership or friendship circle. Whitney et al (1992) believe that victims '...lack the protection against bullying which friendship gives.' (p6). Roy certainly perceived his victimisation as resulting from a lack of identity with a group:

"I didn't really hang around in a gang."

Security was perceived as closely related to being popular and having friends, and Susan perceived that 'being popular' meant:

"Hanging around with the hard lot."

When asked to define 'the hard lot', she stated:

"They go around bullying people."

It would appear that those who were safe from bullying or those who adopted the bullying role were perceived as always being part of a group or having friends. Unlike the victim, they were perceived as never being isolated or alone. This necessity of having group membership and friends seems to play an important part in the informal culture of these pupils in schools. Olweus (1994) believes that bullies usually have two or three supporters who like them and that they are rarely loners. Wayne described bullies as:

"Being in with the crowd."

He described one bully:

"He was never strong, it was the fact that he had three or four people who were bigger than him to back him up."

He added:

"I was never scared of him in the first place, it was just that he had friends."

This statement suggests that bullying is associated with groups of pupils rather than individuals. As Cullingford (1991) observed from his pupil interviews in mainstream; 'Security derives from a sense of cohesion within a group...' (p53). Measor & Woods (1984) revealed that pupils generally felt that having friends around protected them from being bullied and they felt that bullying was less likely to happen when 'your mates are there...' (p14). This may explain Rick's comment that:

"Most new people are bullied."

He perceived there to be a sense of vulnerability that was associated with being isolated and without friends, particularly in a new school environment. However, some pupils felt that to be accepted as part of a group required certain degrees of social conformity, particularly in terms of appearance and behaviour. Whitney et al (1992) suggest that particular characteristics such as clumsiness, dyslexia or other disabilities leave certain pupils vulnerable to victimisation. Susan provided an even broader perspective on this by stating that victims could be:

"People who are really intelligent people. People who are really thick. People who've just got something different about them, that they, the bullies, haven't got."

Cullingford (1993a) agrees stating; '...anything that makes someone stand out is a potential hazard.' (p58). Karen added further support to this argument by stating that the reasons for bullying were:

"Anything, if it's slightly different to anyone else."

Characterisitics of Bullies

Bullies are often part of a group, have many friends and fit certain social norms.

67

George blamed his bullying experience on his surname, which carried a negative personal connotation. His parents had decided to change it yet he perceived his victimisation problems to have started:

"Because of what my name used to be."

Even a simple issue such as wearing glasses could be sufficient to provoke an attack, as Sarah stated:

"Everyone was laughing at me behind my back... and when I started to wear my glasses that was horrible."

Karen offered a slightly different perspective by suggesting that no matter what you wore or what you looked like, if you were not in the majority, the majority being seen as the bullying group, then you would be victimised:

"So it's like it doesn't really matter what you do. If one person's got nice clothes they're gonna pick on you if you've got horrible clothes. Or if they've got horrible clothes they're gonna pick on you if you've got nice clothes. That's why I agree with school uniform."

In certain cases just one specific incident was perceived as being sufficient to trigger bullying. Karen again described an incident that she perceived as having started her own fear of being bullied:

"The teacher was telling a story about a girl getting a needle stuck in her knee. I just went plonk. Apparently I had a fit on the floor and foam was coming out of my mouth ... I was so embarrassed when I woke up, everyone was laughing. I didn't go to school for about a week. I was too scared of what people would say."

Characteristics of Victims

Victims are often seen as not conforming to accepted social norms or are in some way different to other pupils.

Conflicting Research

There is disagreement as to which children adopt bully or victim roles.

The self-esteem and self-image of the victim appears crucial to the development of the role of victim. Many researchers have tried to link certain personalities to victimisation and have used personality theory to explain and explore the types of children who may adopt bully or victim roles, (Mynard & Joseph, 1997). Francis & Jones (1994) comprehensively describe the work carried out in this field in the last twenty years and they list some 'frequently cited descriptions' of victims. These include evidence of depression, anxiety, insecurity, low self-confidence, shyness, preference for own company, few friends, avoidance of social occasions, comparative social isolation. They also describe lower levels of aggressiveness, lower dominance, greater powerlessness and higher sensitivity and submissiveness. Finally they mention lower levels of intelligence and maturity, and often a more positive attitude to school. Interestingly, Olweus (1994) disputes many of these popular theories and suggests that feeling or simply looking different does not result in victimisation instead believing that there is little evidence to support the widely held belief that victimisation is caused by 'external deviations.' (p1178). He turns to personality traits such as anxious, insecure, cautious, sensitive and quiet, as evidence as to who may become a victim. Such people, he maintains, have low self-esteem, are lonely and without friends, and feel unattractive, failures, stupid or ashamed, and he has labelled such victims as passive victims. There is certainly evidence from the pupils with EBD in this present research to support his results and to support the views of Pervin & Turner (1994) who see victims as often blaming themselves for their role. Roy was one such pupil who stated:

"I must have looked irritating to them. They didn't like the way I looked, the way I walked."

George simply stated:

"Like at school everyone didn't like me much."

Another pupil explained the reason for his victimisation:

"I was very very quiet."

Roy's comment perhaps offers support to Olweus' (1994) theory that these victims 'seem to signal to others that they are insecure and worthless individuals, who will not retaliate if they are attacked or insulted.' (p1179). In addition, the height or size of the victim was also perceived as important to a number of the pupils in this study with six pupils in the present study blaming their victimisation on the fact that they were smaller than their bullies:

"I was too small ..."

"I was smaller, they could pick on me and get away with it."

"I don't look my age. I'm small."

"Bullies bully because they're bigger."

"I used to be small. You get shit on."

"I was one of the smallest. I used to be really small."

Following his extensive research, Olweus (1994) confirms that boys who bully are in fact generally physically stronger than average, creating an imbalance in strength or an 'asymmetric power relationship.' (p1173).

However, not all of the victims in this present study were able to give any kind of reason as to why they had been or were being victimised and bullied. They were often unaware of personality traits or aspects of their appearance that may have contributed to their difficulties and were particularly unaware of any behaviours that may have provoked bullying. Olweus (1994) has labelled one type of victim, a provocative victim. He explains; 'These students... behave in ways that may cause irritation and tension around them.' (p1179). Such pupils lose their temper easily and defend themselves when attacked. The statements of some pupils certainly did suggest their role was one of a provocative victim. Mike for example was clearly caught in a cycle of behaviour in which his own response to peer aggression or teasing simply provoked further attack:

Triggers for Victimisation

Low self-esteem, being unusually quiet or small, or having a very short temper may result in victimisation.

"They picked on me because I was the easiest to wind up ... I lost my temper quickly."

Wayne also talked of his retaliation to bullies and recognised that this provoked the bullies further:

"That's how I knew they could get at me."

Despite these comments, pupils such as Wayne tended to adopt descriptions of themselves as passive victims rather than provocative. They rarely perceived their own actions as provocative, preferring to ascribe victimisation to more passive, inescapable reasons, for which they were not responsible.

It seems that we should take a close look into the powerful forces in our society that mould and structure our values and norms, including the media and advertising, which may be playing an important role in the behaviour of our young people in school, and possibly fuelling bullying behaviours. The social norm is an important standard by which the pupils appear to judge themselves and others, and it is often reflected in a competitive attitude to appearance, including clothes. As previously stated pupils perceived that they would be left vulnerable to bullying if they were an outsider and not part of a group, or if they are low in the 'pecking order' of informal sub-cultures that exist within schools. Joining the bullying group was one way to avoid victimisation, yet to become a group member there were certain criteria that first needed to be met. These criteria were described very clearly by certain pupils, including Wayne, who was certain that bullies were:

"Up to date with clothes, big, have friends, going out."

Karen also described what she perceived as the 'competitive' aspect of the social experience of school and the pressure to compete and conform or be isolated and possibly victimised:

"The way you wear your hair, the trainers you've got for PE. It's like so much competition, it's like who's gonna be the best?"

She described why certain pupils might be vulnerable to victimisation:

"If you haven't got the right names on your trainers, or the right labels."

These views were not exclusive to girls; boys were in certain cases equally vulnerable to the pressures of maintaining an acceptable image in the eyes of their peers. Fitting in with the expectations and norms of the peer group was perceived as essential if bullying was to be avoided. Wayne considered that uniform was meant to eliminate such competition but failed:

"Uniform's supposed to be like so everybody wears the same. Doesn't work. People go out and buy £100 blazers and £200 shoes. I just couldn't keep up with it."

70

This perceived pressure to conform to the socially acceptable images of the dominant culture is possibly rooted in the media and its messages. It should be recognised that these messages and their subtle yet powerful influence on young people can have far reaching effects in terms of pupil behaviour in school. Johnny described the importance of his self-image in relation to his ability to conform to school expectations. The seemingly simple issue of the school's requirement for the wearing of a certain type of shoe conflicted with his perception of a socially acceptable image and to Johnny the power and importance of this image outweighed any benefits resulting from conforming to the school rules. Clearly his priorities were very different from those of the school:

> "I ain't gonna learn cause I don't wear shoes ... I don't wear black shoes. They told me to wear them but I still won't wear them. The rest of the uniform is OK its just the shoes. They hurt my feet, and if I get a size bigger they fall off. I look stupid in shoes."

Could these pressures on pupils to maintain an acceptable social image be fuelled by our consumerist society, driven by advertising and the media? Wayne offered evidence for this view:

> "We weren't that well off. Our car wasn't the latest car. We lived in a council house."

This statement illustrates how the victimisation of this pupil involved his personal background and social issues such as the status of his family over which he had little control. For Wayne, his family was certainly a sensitive subject and one frequently chosen by bullies to provoke a victim. Mooney, Creeser & Blatchford (1991) interviewed mainstream pupils and report that a provocative comment would often be aimed at the victim's family or parents. They illustrate their point with a quote from one pupil who explained that it was sufficient to say 'Your Mum' to provoke an attack. (p110). Wayne consistently described this type of teasing or bullying as being an important part of the problems he experienced:

> "They knew how to torment me. It was through my family. My Dad is 65, he's an old man, older than their Grandads even."

Johnny was also aware that his Dad was an older man and told how this had resulted in provocative comments from peers:

> "It really winds me up about my Dad. Taking the Mickey out of my Dad, he's an OAP."

Another concern for certain pupils, was the reputation that they inherited from previous schools. Wayne described feeling trapped within his reputation:

> "The thing is, they knew everything about me cause they've known me all through the years."

He expressed a feeling of helplessness, and an inability to lose the role of victim that had been established. He perceived the only solution to this problem lay in the hands of the authorities and not in changing behaviour:

The Impact of the Media and the Commercial World

The social world of the school is highly competitive and children may be bullied if they do not conform to a media driven socially accepted image.

Expectations Of Family Members

A pupil may be victimised because his or her family members deviate from the norm.

71

"Transfer of school, fresh start, clean start ... where they wouldn't know anything about me."

George also seemed to need a chance for a new identity suggesting that he had experienced bullying because it had become the norm for his peers to behave in that way towards him. In a new environment he felt he would escape the victimisation because those around him would not be familiar with him in that role:

"I suppose they wouldn't know what everyone, how everyone treated me before."

Karen saw the answer lying, not just in moving schools, but in the family moving away to live in a new area:

Carrying a Reputation

Certain pupils feel unable to lose their role of or reputation as a victim.

"I think if we moved and went to a different area."

This issue and some of the comments are developed and discussed further in chapter 4 when the pupils' perceptions are used to gain a better understanding of behaviours which result from labelling and reputations. These rather desperate statements by pupils appear to reflect a loss of hope in the schools themselves or the supportive people in their lives being able to prevent bullying. In many cases they were disillusioned with the ability of schools to prevent or deal with negative social interaction and often spoke clearly about aspects of school and schooling that did little to help them with these issues. In fact they described various aspects of schools and schooling processes that they perceived as having nurtured their social problems.

The school environment and bullying

This section describes the pupils' perceptions of situations or processes within the school that may have contributed to negative social interaction with their peers. There is a close relationship between these perceptions and class and school size or teachers and teaching. For example bullying is perceived by some pupils in this study as being a result of the large numbers of pupils both in the school as a whole and in classrooms, with insufficient staff to monitor and oversee activities. Bobby had resigned himself to the fact that bullying would happen as a consequence of the number of pupils in one place:

Large Schools and Classes

Large numbers of pupils in schools and classes may create opportunities for bullying.

"There's so many people, it's bound to happen."

Additionally, the nature and layout of the school building had also created difficulties for a minority of pupils and for some of the pupils this aspect of schools had led to intense anxiety. A small number of pupils felt physically threatened by peers as a result of the institutional nature of the buildings and the mass movement of pupils through the building at certain times of the day. This comment made by Roy describes such a situation:

"They run through the school, knocking all the 1st years over. It was scary."

72

Dave was another pupil who felt vulnerable as a result of the number of pupils in the schools and congestion resulting from overcrowded areas:

"Too big. You couldn't hardly move in the corridors. You had to squeeze past them."

Jeremy also commented:

"I couldn't cope with school. Just being around everybody. The school was cramped."

It appeared that a number of pupils associated high numbers of pupils in schools with inadequate supervision, feeling that much bullying occurred when and where teachers could not see it. Siann, Callaghan, Lockhart & Rawson (1993) stress the importance of high quality supervision in improving school ethos and reduction of bullying incidents. However, even with the best intentions and supervision plans, the ability of teachers to be aware of all social activity may be limited and it is perhaps unrealistic to expect them to see all bullying incidents. There certainly does seem to be evidence for a mismatch between how pupils experience the nature and extent of bullying in a school, compared to the perceptions of teachers. Pervin & Turner (1994) investigated staff and pupil knowledge, attitudes and beliefs about bullying in one inner city school, and revealed high numbers of pupils reporting experiences of bullying, yet lower teacher awareness. Galloway (1994) supports this by quoting that there is 'extensive evidence that teachers do not get to hear about the majority of bullying in the schools.' (p21). It may be, as Cullingford (1993a) proposes, that owing to inadequate supervision, the majority of bullying behaviour '...takes place out of the sight of teachers,' (p57). However, pupils have suggested other explanations for a lack of support, including that reporting incidents to teachers was not an effective means of controlling the problem or being safe. In such cases they had elected not to involve their teachers at all, feeling that teachers had no idea how to deal with bullying or trivialised incidents and therefore ignored any complaints. Other pupils perceived their teachers' support as simply making social situations worse. Karen voiced her disappointment and frustration at the lack of support offered by one teacher after she had reported bullying incidents in a class:

"I'd go and tell Mr. Jones, he'd just say 'Oh well, ignore them'."

This kind of advice had also been offered to Wayne who was adamant that it was not possible to ignore bullies and that this was not a means of dealing with bullies, despite what teachers or other adults might suggest:

"Rubbish. Not possible. They just carry on and on until you break."

He also added that just shrugging off bullying was:

"One of the most impossible things you can really do."

Karen also described an incident when acid had been thrown at her in a science class but on reporting it to the teacher was told:

Building Design and Pupil Schedules

Mass movement of pupils between classes and through institutionalised buildings may exacerbate aggressive behaviours.

"Well it wasn't that strong anyway."

Mike experienced a similar lack of concern from teachers:

"I didn't used to do anything. I used to leave it with the teachers who usually didn't sort it...."

Karen proposed that fear was the reason behind her teacher adopting such a passive stance to her problem:

"...I think he was scared of the other people as well."

This interesting insight illustrates the fact that pupils may not be alone in experiencing the fear or insecurity created by bullying. Teachers may also experience anxiety or uncertainty if they lack the support, clear strategies and skills needed to confidently deal with aggressive behaviour. Boulton (1997) explored teachers' views on bullying and found that they '...were not confident in their ability to deal with bullying and 87 per cent wanted more training.' (p223). Cullingford (1991) reports of finding pupils with little expectation of support from many teachers and those who mentioned bullying seemed to assume that teachers would not take the problem seriously, even if they wanted to. Of course it is also possible that teachers genuinely do not perceive the incidents reported to them as important, or simply do not have the time to deal with them.

Much research on bullying in the last 10 to 15 years has involved asking the pupils themselves for their perceptions and experiences and this has allowed comparisons to be made with the perceptions of professionals. Branwhite (1994) for example states that first year secondary pupils describe things that create stress very differently from parents and professional. This may account for the attitudes of certain teachers towards reports of bullying and their apparent unwillingness to offer support. They may not perceive certain situations as requiring their intervention, being unaware of the degree of stress being experienced by certain pupils.

Some pupils in this and similar studies proposed a further reason why teachers may be unaware of the extent of bullying. These pupils were concerned that reporting incidents to teachers would lead to punishments for bullies that would have no effect on their behaviour:

"The head actually went into class ... he said to the kids how would you feel if you were being bullied by him and all his friends. They all said 'Yeh, Yeh' .... but as soon as they got outside the lesson it just started again."

Wayne also felt that punishments for bullies were ineffective and made this resigned comment:

"Whatever they did, they'd come back and do it again."

Roy was very despondent about the possibility of stopping bullying in the school:

"No they can't stop it, can't stamp it out. Bullies are like ants, you kill one off, there's the other one running away, and you get that one and there's another one. Can't be stamped out."

However, of even greater concern than the ineffectiveness or futility of punishment was that it would actually increase the level of bullying and that there would be repercussions resulting from the involvement of teachers and the punishment of the bully. Robinson and Maines (1997) discuss these problems in some detail. Pervin & Turner (1994) propose fear of revenge, intimidation or lack of confidentiality as reasons for pupils not reporting incidents to teachers more frequently, and pupils in this present study strongly supported these proposals. Wayne was one pupil who made comments to this effect:

"Trying to punish them just made them more angry with me."

He added further detail:

"She got these people doing litter duty. She was trying to punish them but she's stupid ... it made them more angry with me."

Michael and Roy had similar perceptions and had chosen to deal with their difficulties alone:

"I hit 'em back. I didn't bother telling... I'd get my head kicked in."

"I didn't wanna tell the teachers, cause they don't care, they tell 'em off, and it just gets worse and worse. Then there's no point."

Three pupils who had witnessed bullying yet were not involved themselves, also expressed this fear of seeking support. Their statements illustrate the potential consequences of reporting on others, or 'grassing', which was perceived as an unwise thing to do for fear of reprisal:

"I didn't wanna grass on anyone."

"I didn't know if I told on them whether they'd come back and have a go at me."

"Richard spread rumours that I was a grass. They started to have a go at me."

Clearly this is an important issue that schools should consider when tackling bullying. It appears from the perceptions of these pupils that inadequate management of social problems such as bullying in school may be pushing threatening behaviours under the surface, making them less visible to staff. Pupils experiencing bullying may in fact be placed in situations where they simply do not know what to do. (Sharp, 1995). If as Cullingford (1993) states from his research with mainstream pupils that; '...in children's eyes teachers will not or cannot cope with the problem.' (p57), then they will be forced to adopt their own survival strategies. The comments made by pupils with EBD in the present study suggest that their survival strategies could be the behaviours that

Inadequate Support from Teachers

Teachers may not observe bullying directly.

Teachers may be inadequately trained to deal with bullying.

Teachers may trivialise bullying.

Teachers' responses may exacerbate problems.

Teachers may not have the time to deal with bullying.

Survival Strategies

Pupils with EBD appear to lack appropriate behavioural skills for dealing with bullying.

escalate their problems. These pupils may be unable to meet and find a balance between the social demands of the school and acceptable behaviours. Their behavioural choices appear limited to suffering, avoiding a victim role, or joining the aggressors. This issue will be discussed in more detail in chapter 4 but the following brief comments illustrate the ability of the pupils to justify their behaviour in terms of survival. George explained the choices he had made in his mainstream school:

> "We used to hang around with the bullies, they don't turn around and bully you so we used to hang around with bullies."

Karen had been able to analyse her own and the behaviour of others in some depth:

> "If someone's picking on someone they go with the bully not with the victim. Maybe it's because they're scared because they're gonna do something to them…"

She described how she herself had participated in bullying at one time, giving the reason as:

> "Everyone knew if you weren't with her you got beaten up by her."

Olweus (1994) has referred to this type of bully as a passive bully, henchman or follower, (p1180). Karen described joining in with a girl who bullied, but considered it to be unlike her usual behaviour:

> "It's like if you saw someone in the street you'd carry on with her. It's like I didn't know what I was doing at the time, and afterwards I thought 'why the hell did I do that? It's not what I'd usually do.'"

Competition in Schools

Competitive practices in schools may encourage aggressive behaviours.

In addition to the inability of teachers to satisfactorily prevent or deal with incidents of bullying, it is also important to be aware of the ways in which schools may inadvertently encourage or nurture bullying through their day to day practices involving competition, discipline, and adult models of bullying. A small number of pupils commented on these aspects of schools including Tom, a 14 year old boy at the Oakwood Centre who provided an interesting statement concerning competitive grouping of pupils:

> "Because he was really getting on my nerves, and he was on the other side. Like we had Vikings, Saxons and Normans, he said something nasty to me so I hit him."

Besag (1989) believes that competitive attitudes to education can provide a legitimate opportunity to generate inferiority or distress. She describes '…a highly competitive approach to academic, sporting or social success, which by intent makes others feel inferior or causes distress.' (p4). As previously described in this chapter, PE was certainly an unpopular subject for a number of pupils and a possible reason for this is given by Arnold (1994) who describes football for boys as providing 'a screen for high levels of negative coercive behaviour: competition and rivalry between the boys … , physical and verbal abuse within the game itself...' (p185). If this is true then we should be aware that some schooling activities may actually encourage behaviours that would readily fall into the majority of broad definitions of bullying.

Adult models of bullying related to discipline have been described to some extent earlier in the chapter where pupils' perceptions of teacher aggression were presented. Arnold (1994) proposes that adults in schools may model bullying by shouting and giving autocratic commands which interestingly was one of the behaviours that pupils in this present study most frequently claimed to dislike in teachers. Perhaps we can in fact view many attempts at discipline within a school as examples of bullying. From his observations inside schools, Galloway (1994) considers that those schools with the highest rates of bullying were the most likely to deal with bullying by corporal punishment. Ironically, it is possible that even a well-intentioned anti-bullying policy may unwittingly contradict its own goals if methods of discipline within it are not carefully scrutinised. Clearly the whole issue of discipline within schools and the way punitive measures are implemented may have strong implications for the way pupils behave, inadvertently offering models of legitimate bullying. Ways must be found to deal with bullying that do not involve actions that effectively model and legitimise aggressive behaviours (Robinson and Maines,1997). Support for all concerned may be the only truly effective approach (Young, 1998).

Teachers may also need to recognise that their relationships with pupils can create some fears similar to those experienced through bullying by peers. Certain behaviours that are most commonly associated with negative pupil interaction may also occur between teachers and pupils. For example, being 'picked on' is a common phrase associated with both playground bullying and classroom experience. These experiences of being singled out and isolated unfairly from the group, readily fall under most broad definitions of bullying. One pupil stated:

> "I used to get it from the teachers too. If I was sitting in the class and someone was talking, I used to get the blame for it."

Mooney et al (1991) describe teasing or 'taking the Mickey' as another behaviour that does not occur only amongst pupils, although the pupils in this present study described it as being primarily between peers. It is important to recognise that the expressions 'teasing' and 'being picked on' can very easily be interchanged with the word 'bullying' and certain actions involving adults or pupils in a school can upset pupils with EBD. For example, one pupil made this comment about his teachers:

> "They always picked on me, not others."

Galloway (1994) suggests that bullying between pupils cannot be tackled in isolation and takes the issue of bullying beyond pupil interaction alone, suggesting that all types of relationships within a school influence each other. If bullying is a learned behaviour as Galloway suggests, and learning takes place in all aspects of schooling and society as a whole, then the issue of bullying may be closely linked to the behaviour of adults in society, including schools. If this is the case it therefore becomes a community problem and not the

Adult Models of Bullying

Certain discipline practices may model bullying.

Teachers singling out pupils and teasing them may be perceived as bullying by sensitive pupils.

Bullying as a Whole Community Problem

Bullying in schools may be a reflection of adult behaviours in schools and across society.

responsibility of schools alone (Randall, 1996). Robinson and Maines (1997) develop this theme of bullying in society and give a detailed account of how a Headteacher may bully staff and pupils. Perhaps bullying behaviours have become so much the norm within schools and even within society as a whole, that we barely recognise them or their impact. However, the pupils with EBD in this study were certainly deeply affected by such behaviours and appear to be a very special group for whom the nature of social relationships within schools is of extreme importance.

Motives for bullying

Pupils who were themselves bullies and also those who had been victimised were equally able to contribute comments regarding motives for bullying behaviour. Those who had been victims included Jeremy and also Chris, a 13 year old boy at Southdown with learning difficulties who had become a school refuser following incidents of bullying in his mainstream school. These boys held the following perceptions regarding the motives of their attackers:

> "To get a thrill. Some people get an adrenaline rush off cars, motor-bikes, some people get it out of bullying, smoking, stuff like that."

> "Some people do it for a laugh."

> "They just hit for pleasure."

Ken perceived that the bullies gained more than a simple pleasure or thrill from their actions. His own personal analysis had led him to believe that:

> "It makes them feel good about themselves, makes them look big and tough."

These perceptions are in close agreement with those of the mainstream pupils interviewed in previous studies who gave reasons for teasing as enjoyment and also prestige for the teaser. Pupils in the present study also described provocation as another reason for bullying, often using the term being 'wound up' by bullies. Mike was clear that the motive behind the bullying that he had seen and experienced was:

> "To wind people up."

Simon agreed and also emphasised the repetitive nature of such behaviour:

> "People pick on one kid for a week, just digging him, digging him."

Wayne also perceived that bullies would continue provocation until the victim gave the desired response. He explained:

> "I've been told they know you're getting upset by it. If I could just ignore it they wouldn't. Rubbish. I tried it. It don't work. They just carry on and carry on until you break. You can't ignore it that long. Impossible."

The pupils' comments certainly do suggest that bullies have a desire to provoke their victim until a reaction is secured and that desired reaction is often an aggressive retaliation. Chris described how he responded:

> "If he called me names, I tried ignoring it until a certain point... then I retaliated, nearly knocked his ... done the same to him as he done to me."

Interestingly, this illustrates how the victim may ultimately display greater physical aggression than the bully. In these cases it may be the victim who is disciplined by the school while the more covert tactics of the aggressor are overlooked. Certainly the expression 'being wound up' was used by a significant number of the pupils to describe their feelings or to justify their actions. Johnny believed that the aim of the bully was to wind up their victims until the victim responded aggressively and was then 'in trouble':

> "They would try and wound you up very badly so you're the one who gets in trouble."

Both Neil and Karl, a 16 year old boy at the Oakwood Centre, commented:

> "He would wind me up so much to the point where he was asking to be hit. Sometimes I would just lose my rag."

> " ... but most of the time I get provoked. I'm easily wound up."

The art of provocation or 'winding up' appeared to often rely on the ability to identify and probe the victim's weak, sensitive inner core of values. As previously described, pupils often perceived these as being related to some aspect of their family and Karl and Wayne both commented on this:

> "Somebody might say something about my Mum and I'd say 'what you saying?' "

> "I'd stick up for my parents and my brother."

Susan also explained her reaction to such provocation:

> "And one time [she] turned round and said something about my Mum and Dad or something ... I wasn't in a particularly good mood that day, so I turned round and I got a chair and I lugged it at her."

Provocation also appeared to have other goals in addition to seeking a physically aggressive response. Tom, a very small boy, was provoked into stealing by comments that clearly touched his inner insecurity:

> "They started calling me a wimp and a chicken so I nicked a bar of chocolate because they told me to."

It may be that both the need to provoke and the need to respond or retaliate have their roots in a child protecting self-esteem. According to the values of

Why Bullies Bully

Reasons for bullying given by pupils include: fun, pleasure, adrenaline, provocation, to feel better, to get others into trouble.

many pupil subcultures or groups within schools, protecting one's self esteem may necessitate aggressive or antisocial behaviour. If the response to bullying is aggressive, then the ability to distinguish the bully from the victim in terms of observed behaviour may be marred, creating problems for those dealing with such problems. Given the large percentage of pupils describing retaliation as their reason for aggressive behaviour, it seems crucial that professionals look closely at such behaviours to ensure an adequate understanding of their pupils' difficulties. As Simon explained, aggressive behaviour creates a vicious circle for certain pupils:

> "It's passed on. If it's happened to me then I'll do it. Eventually you get pushed so far you turn round and do it back."

Tom supported this belief:

> "People bully because they get bullied themselves."

Bully or Victim?

Some victims may become bullies.

Some pupils who had bullied younger weaker children gave their reason as being a reaction to the fact that they themselves had been bullied by older or stronger pupils, to whom they had not had the courage to retaliate. This suggests that certain bullies could be gaining something from their actions that does not involve impressing their peer group. The bullying of younger children or siblings does not appear to be an effective way of enhancing self-esteem or status within their own peer group. This suggests that in certain cases bullying is more than purely an activity aimed at improving one's social image and self-esteem related to a group. Instead, it may be associated with a more personal, inner need. Danny described such behaviour:

> "People push them around, and they can't hit 'em back so they start on little ones."

The following statement by Wayne illustrates the confusion and frustration that can be felt by some pupils when trying to find acceptable behavioural options with which to respond to bullying:

> "I battled it. I had a go at them. I couldn't hit 'em cause I'd get in trouble, so when I had a go at them I'd swear and stuff. That's how I knew they could get at me, getting me into that state. That's why I got into trouble, if they hit me, I'd hit 'em back, then I got into trouble."

Although certain pupils described their attempts at avoiding confrontation and conforming to the rules of the school, they perceived this lack of retaliation as threatening their status and self-esteem. As Measor & Woods (1984) state; 'Once more it is status ...that is at stake.' (p12). Retaliation is clearly as much an attempt to protect one's emotions or ego as it is concerned with physical survival. Jeremy described the importance of being able to 'look after' himself:

> "I don't like fighting but if I have to I will. I can look after myself if I have to."

'Looking after' oneself may have physical or emotional implications, with the possibility of needing to look after one's fragile self-esteem being equally if not more important than looking after one's physical well-being. George's self-esteem and status amongst his peers was clearly low, as revealed by previous statements. He described how he had aggressively responded to constant invitations to fight as if it was his only way to emotionally survive the torment:

> "They just gang up and say do you wanna fight ... Everyone was saying like 'go on George you can do him easy', so I did."

The statements made by the pupils in this study suggest that there may be a significant number of pupils who are currently being labelled as EBD as a result of aggressive behaviours that may start as self-defence. In many cases such behaviour appears to be fuelled by a particularly fragile ego and low self-esteem possibly relating to, or created by, complex personal and social issues:

> "Then I started to fight back, and I hit a boy in my class."

> "Yeh, if they took the Mickey out of me, I used to bash everyone, and get in more and more trouble."

> "He used to tell lies about me. One day I went up to him and smacked his head against the radiator."

> "Because they were annoying me, annoying me all day, and at dinner time, when all his friends started to annoy me, I went up to him and just hit him. I nearly killed him."

It is difficult for professionals to assess the extent to which aggressive behaviour is simply pre-empting a possible attack, or attempting to deter future or more serious attacks by peers. Where aggression has put down its roots in a school, fear breeds further fear and further aggression. As Boulton (1993b) suggests, if the child does respond aggressively to teasing it 'might deter the perpetrator from teasing them in the future or from using more serious forms of attack.' (p242). Tom added strength to this suggestion by stating that to avoid being bullied:

> "You have to be a good fighter."

Some pupils clearly felt justified in responding to certain situations with aggression and in some cases pupils perceived this view to also be held by their parents and other adult figures. Such encouragement clearly creates confusion for young people who are faced with conflicting expectations and values in school and at home. For pupils with EBD, finding appropriate responses to stressful situations may be difficult as their personal value systems can be fragile and potentially vulnerable to the values of more significant individuals and groups around them. Certain pupils described their own aggressive or threatening behaviour as being influenced by peers, including Bobby who felt that his behaviour was very different when he was with people than when alone:

Self Defence

Aggressive behaviours may be perceived by pupils as self-defence.

81

"I think it was the kids I mixed with. When I'm on my own I'm alright ... it's just when I get around people, bad people."

John also described getting involved with the 'wrong crowd' and perceived the influence of a bad group of peers as the reason for his anti-social behaviour:

"I used to hang around a lot with all the people who weren't the right people to hang around with."

The Influence of Others

Parents, adults and peers may all actually encourage aggression in different ways.

It appears that this pressure to become a part of the dominant peer group in a school was certainly an important issue for these pupils with EBD. Additionally there was insight into the fact that a small number of pupils had adopted bullying behaviour having previously been victims. Ivan, a 15 year old boy at Southdown who had been expelled from mainstream school for disruptive behaviour, explained:

"I used to get picked on by some of the older kids. When those kids left I got on, and I started bullying a bit, with kids of my age."

Rick also explained how he had changed from victim to aggressor:

"I used to be bullied, that's why I bully now I think ... you just pass it on."

Mooney et al (1991) found that envy was one of the reasons given by pupils for teasing. Ronnie described his own reluctance to work in class and his subsequent actions that were intended to prevent the achievements of others:

"I banged their fingers on the tables so they couldn't get on with the work any more."

Self Worth

Bullying may be an attempt to raise feelings of self worth.

It is certainly tempting to suggest that aggressive bullying behaviour is strongly linked to a pupil's need to dominate others in order to boost his or her own feelings of self-worth. Ronnie made an interesting statement to this effect, stating:

"I'm the Daddy of the school."

However, although Olweus (1994) describes a need for power and dominance (p1180) as one of the psychological motivational sources underlying bullying, he interestingly claims to have found little evidence to support the common view of bullies, that they have low self-esteem and are anxious and insecure. The reason for this misconception could be linked to the difficulty that exists in discerning who the actual bully is, which was discussed earlier in this chapter. Many pupils who display aggressive, bullying behaviours may simply be responding to provocation, or attempting to pre-empt attack. If this is the case, then their underlying motives for bullying may be quite different from those of a pupil whose personality or needs actually initiate an aggressive encounter. However, bullying does seem to be closely linked to issues of self-esteem, although much behaviour remains open to interpretation, particularly if the pupils themselves are given little opportunity to discuss this issue with professionals, including teachers. If bullying is playing a significant role in the

Interpreting Behaviour

Understanding the true meaning of behaviour is difficult but essential in helping pupils with EBD.

behaviours of pupils with EBD, as this study suggests, then it is obviously essential that the perceptions of these pupils are actively sought and that they are encouraged to analyse and discuss their own behaviours.

Key points emerging from this section

- Pupils face significant challenges related to the social aspects of schooling.

- Pupils with EBD are often unable to cope with the social challenges within a mainstream school and perceive a lack of support from staff.

- Pupils with EBD often lack appropriate or adequate behavioural options for dealing with social pressures and thus resort to disturbing or unacceptable behaviours.

- Attempts at dealing with bullies and bullying within schools are often ineffective and overly punitive.

Thoughts for your reflection

- Are you aware of the aspects of your school or classroom that may nurture bullying?

- Be wary of highly competitive practices in your school or classroom instruction that may legitimise or encourage aggressive actions or attitudes.

- What do you do to prevent bullying in your school or classroom?

- Are you truly effective when trying to deal with incidents or reports of bullying?

- Are you alert to the wide range of behaviours that constitute bullying?

- Do you really listen to children who report bullying?

- Have you carefully considered your own behaviours to ensure that you are not modelling any bullying type behaviours?

- Have you explored the variety of approaches to bullying that are now being proposed and organized training for yourself or your staff?

Tips for improving your success with difficult or challenging children

- Make yourself available for children to talk to you about their concerns and anxieties.

- Be aware that your perception of an incident or a particular child may be different from that of your pupils.

- Make sure that the bully you see is not the victim reacting.

- Believe in and listen to what your pupils have to say and accept that bullying can be very extensive.

- Do not under play or trivialise any incidents of bullying.

- Be aware that bullying takes many forms and not all are openly visible or physical in nature.

- Try to be particularly alert to the problems facing children with EBD as they may be more vulnerable as victims or inclined to bully.

- Pupils with EBD may not have developed behavioural skills for dealing with challenging social situations and therefore need support.

- Be alert at all times to the social interaction of pupils in your classroom particularly when the class is very large.

- Try to limit or effectively monitor the mass movement of pupils around the school.

- Deal with bullies in a way that will not exacerbate the problem for the victim. Think of a way to avoid blame. (Robinson and Maines, 1997, Young, 1998)

- Be aware that a sensitive child may misconstrue your playful teasing.

- Be sensitive to the fact that the attitudes and behaviours of parents may confuse their children with regards to what are acceptable behaviours.

- Take care that you do not use discipline techniques that model aggression or bullying or that your relationships with your staff or colleagues are not abusive.

- Seek appropriate training and materials for successful prevention and intervention when bullying arises and ensure that a policy exists both in your classroom and school.

3.1 (v) **Bringing it all together**

There is a danger that some mainstream schools or teachers may not wish to consider certain pupils to be their responsibility, perhaps feeling themselves unable to meet those children's needs adequately. Johnny recalled a comment made by one of his teachers in the mainstream school that may illustrate the significance of this point:

> "I told them, 'can you slow down a bit?' and he didn't. He said you 'shouldn't be at this school then.' My hands were hurting."

However, this section concerning schools and teachers does reveal the potentially significant role that mainstream schools and teachers can play in supporting pupils with EBD in that setting. Some of the most important conclusions that emerge from the pupils' comments in this section are as follows:

- Schools themselves do have an important role to play in shaping the behaviours of pupils with EBD and subsequently the success or failure of those children in mainstream education.

- Schools place extreme academic, social and emotional demands on pupils which when combined with other factors can manifest themselves in challenging or difficult behaviours.

- A variety of factors and processes within schools, such as school and class size, teacher/pupil ratios, teacher behaviours and practices, curriculum content and social interactions, can combine to create or nurture difficulties for children.

- Pupils with EBD appear to struggle with the challenges they face in schools, possibly lacking the behavioural options or skills necessary to survive and have their needs met.

- With careful consideration and sensitivity to the needs of challenging pupils, schools and teachers can make a difference to the success of pupils with EBD.

3.2 **Families and life outside school**

This section presents the pupils' perceptions of factors outside school, which they perceived as having influenced their behaviour. These include factors associated with their families and personal biographies, and also their socioeconomic and sociocultural experiences. A number of the pupils interviewed in the study felt that their lives out of school had presented them with difficulties that they perceived as having contributed in some way to their behaviours relating to school, and their subsequent placement in special education.

Much research has been carried out and published regarding the contribution that family and parenting experiences have made to children's behaviour, and the association between social class and culture and anti-social, disruptive or deviant behaviour. Charlton & David (1989) describe and discuss the large amount of research that has been carried out into the impact of factors such as parental separation, inadequate parenting, bereavement, abuse, disturbed family, divorce and social class differences. They clearly demonstrate the extent of interest in this issue, yet overall the results of such study often remain inconclusive. There is certainly disagreement and evidence of inconsistencies, particularly in attempting to associate socioeconomic factors with behaviour, although links between behaviour in school and stressful family or home backgrounds are often harder to dispute. Even as far back as the 1940's, (Wills, 1941, 1945), attempts were made to link learning difficulties and maladjustment to personal problems resulting largely from family disturbance. More recently the influence of schooling itself, as described previously, has been recognised and researched, yet as Charlton & David (1989) state, family

Research

The impact of children's family or social experiences on their behaviour has attracted much research.

85

influence is still unavoidably an important issue for special needs pupils. '...the range, duration and quality of family experiences are likely to make significant contributions, adversely or otherwise, to children's behaviour.' (p24).

The early researchers, eagerly pursuing the use of positivist styles of investigation into this issue, were certainly confident in linking the nature of the family, or its social class, to the behaviour of disruptive children. In the 1960's and 1970's links between home background, including socioeconomic status, and the child's success or failure in school, were eagerly pursued. As Galloway & Goodwin (1987) state; 'Until the mid 1960's tensions arising from family background and from disturbed relationships within the family were seen as the principal cause of maladjustment.'(p46). They state how personal, child centred problems, were the focus for most maladjustment and learning difficulties, and such problems were closely associated with family composition and difficulties and also social class. Upton (1983) describes research that considers these factors and reveals a high degree of agreement as to their significance. Such a focus was a move towards recognising that social and family pressures could influence a child's behaviour, which was an important step away from the more traditional medical, psychiatric or psychodynamic theories of behaviour, which stress the importance of unconscious processes within the individual. Yet these new correlations and patterns that were being sought still fell short of exploring the possible interaction between internal and external processes that were associated with behaviours. In other words, they were concerned with correlation but not cause. They may have created a general awareness of the different environmental factors affecting a pupil but still largely supported the belief that maladjustment and problem behaviours were products of external impact on the child. There remained little belief or concern with the ability of the pupil to make decisions about his/her own behaviour or to be able to express motives for behaviour.

Finding Causes of Disturbing Behaviour

Behaviourist research has exposed correlations between family variables and school problems.

The discovery of correlations between social variables and behaviour challenged traditional medical models for understanding behaviour.

Such behaviourist research has continued through the 1980's and into the early 1990's despite the parallel development of more humanistic research into interactionist theories of behaviour. Galloway & Goodwin (1987) quote research into social class distribution within schools for the maladjusted, with results showing that the majority of children were from social class 4 and 5. Family composition was also investigated and it was revealed that for the pupils in three schools for the maladjusted 22.5% of cases had fathers who were dead, absent or unknown. Other work linking class to disruption and truancy includes Davie, Butler and Goldstein (1972) and Farrington (1980), and there is a great deal of other research that reveals patterns and correlation between the behaviour of pupils with EBD and social variables.

The pioneers of humanistic research included Rogers and Maslow in the 1960's, as described in Cooper (1989). The true concerns of this group of researchers only slowly emerged in the 1970's and 1980's when the value of the statistical evidence from the behaviourists was questioned in favour of a consideration of the uniqueness of the individual. Thus the humanists strove to look beyond correlations within data into why the patterns were appearing and began to investigate the nature of the behaviour as a rational response to certain conflicting social pressures and circumstances. Conflicts between home life, the child's socio-cultural value systems and the values and expectations of the school, as possible causes for disruptive behaviour, began to be considered. There was increasing knowledge regarding the subcultures of deviant pupils, both in and out of school, and the values associated with these cultures. Deviance was also being strongly proposed as being a result of formal or informal pupil cultures existing in schools. These proposals included the pro-school and anti-school cultures revealed by researchers such as Hargreaves (1967) and Lacey (1970), which were strongly related to social class and are described in Woods (1983). Willis (1977) argued slightly differently on the same theme, that pupils do in fact have well established cultural values and ties based on their social class backgrounds that do not evolve from a conflict with school, yet contribute to failure within school. Bird, Chessum, Furlong & Johnson (1981) actually showed from a pupil perspective that cultural values alien to those of the school were important in the rejection of or disaffection with school displayed by certain pupils.

The work of Rutter et al (1979), investigating the role of the school itself in the failure of certain pupils, brought the school under the spotlight and school variables began to be considered alongside family or social variables. This research into the importance of schooling factors began to reveal that a highly complex combination of factors might influence pupil behaviour. Although the developing spotlight on the school did not displace the importance of psychological and sociological factors, certain results did put a question mark over some of the previous research. Interestingly, Rutter et al (1979) found no relationship between pupils' behaviour within London secondary schools and their social backgrounds. Similarly, Galloway et al (1982) could find no direct correlation between exclusion rates in secondary schools and the social class of their pupil intake. In 1994 he maintains this belief (Galloway, 1994) and stresses the importance of avoiding making simple statements regarding correlations between behaviour and social variables in the child's background stating:

'It is by now well established that schools vary widely in the prevalence of disruptive behaviour and that these variations cannot be attributed simply to the social background of the pupils they admit.' (p20).

Similarly Charlton & David (1989) suggest that it is risky to always link disadvantaged homes with disturbed children. However, such statements must contend with past and continuing research. In a National Child Development Study, Wedge & Essen (1982) found a relationship between family disadvantage and educational attainment, where disadvantage was defined as; (1) Had only one parent and/or five or more children, (2) Lived in an overcrowded house or a house with no hot water, and (3) Received means-tested welfare benefits on account of their low income. More recently other work continues to produce significant evidence to reinforce such correlation. Ashford (1994) refers to media coverage which claimed that the make-up of the family was directly linked to potential exclusion from school. According to this research, children from single parent families or families with a step-parent were more likely to suffer a range of health, behavioural and educational problems. For example a reconstituted family was reported as being ten times more likely to have a child with behavioural problems, and a one parent family, twice as likely than a nuclear family. Ashford's own research in rural comprehensive schools reinforced these findings, by showing that there were indeed greater

Humanistic Research

The uniqueness of the individual was considered important by humanistic researchers.

Cultural values and the existence of pupil subcultures in schools have been investigated in relation to behaviour.

How the School can Influence Behaviour

Research focussing on schools and schooling processes challenged previously accepted correlations between social factors and behaviour in school.

More Evidence of Correlations

Research continues to link social variables to school attainment.

numbers of exclusions from one parent or reconstituted families in these schools. Further evidence is provided by Olweus (1994) who includes family factors and in particular parenting styles in his conclusions as to where aggressive bullying behaviours are rooted. He refers to negative emotional attitudes of the child, a lack of clear limits being set by the caretaker, and the use of power assertive child rearing methods, such as physical punishment and violent emotional outbursts. (p1182). He does however state clearly that he finds only a very weak relationship between these childhood factors and the socio-economic conditions of the family, which is an important consideration.

The Interaction of Variables

Quantitative analysis seeking simple correlation between variables may overlook the complexity of the interaction of these variables and their impact on behaviour.

It would appear that research that attempts to investigate which family and social factors may contribute to a child's behaviour, provides greater opportunity for quantitative, statistical data than research into school based factors, which are often less tangible. Yet although correlation between social background or family structure and success in school may be measurable, the variables are often so closely linked that such research does need careful interpretation. The development of interactionist theories of behaviour have encouraged a closer look at this interaction of variables and has helped to illustrate the way in which different factors, including school, may combine to maintain or even nurture inequalities based within the social background of the child. Additionally, they have encouraged the belief that individuals do in fact try to make sense of all interacting social systems, and for this reason it is of value to try to investigate the perception of the individual if we are to fully understand behaviour.

Using the Pupils' Perspective

There appears to be limited educational research seeking pupils' perspectives of how social variables impact their behaviour.

Interestingly however, although researchers continue to debate the importance of social background and family life in the success or failure of school pupils, little interest has been shown in the pupils' own perceptions of this issue. Unlike investigations into the role of the schools themselves and schooling factors, for which there has been an upsurge in interest in what the pupils think, (Ruddock et al, 1995, Davies, 1996), the pupils' perceptions of the importance of their family life and social backgrounds as factors contributing to their behavioural difficulties appears to have been less of a focus. Investigations of a therapeutic nature may reveal children's own subjective attitudes and views regarding the impact of these out of school factors on their difficulties and behaviour, but educational research attempting to assess the relative importance of these factors for a pupil with EBD from their perspective, is apparently scarce. One recent piece of statistical research, Branwhite (1994), does however describe work carried out in five overseas countries with nearly two thousand children aged between 8 and 14, who were questioned regarding sources of stress. Interestingly, it was reported that 90% of the participants described experience of family discord and many of the pupils ranked parent related stressors higher than school related stresses.

In the study described in this book, pupils were given the opportunity to discuss or describe anything out of school that had affected their school life and behaviour. Seventeen of the pupils made statements which suggested that their school difficulties were in some way linked to family or broader social issues, although of these, many described school factors in addition. This clearly indicates the interactive nature of the factors for the pupils, and again highlights the difficulty in attempting to isolate significant factors.

Loss of parents

In agreement with Montgomery (1989) and Frude in Fontana (1985), a small number of pupils in the present study described family breakdown as being disturbing to them and influencing their behaviour. Robert spoke very little in the interviews and apparently had been reluctant even in therapy to attempt to address his problems. He did however state:

> "I think it was when my father left the problems started."

Beyond this statement he was unable or unwilling to elaborate on how or why this event had affected him. Johnny also made statements which gave a clear indication of the perception of the role his parents' divorce had played in his difficulties:

> "If my Mum had stayed with us I'd have been in normal school now. My Mum would make sure we were in school. I'd have been alright at school if my Mum had been there."

Johnny was certainly frustrated by the loss of his Mum and stated clearly and simply the emotional problems that this loss created for him:

> "I didn't want my Mum to leave, definitely not. Things ain't going well now since she left ... I tell my Mum that I want her back but she doesn't listen. I say things aren't working with me and me Dad, having arguments all the time ... she doesn't do anything about it."

He continued with a description of some of the simple, practical problems that the loss had created for him that affected his social life within the school:

> "I was unsettled then. I was used to my Mum's cooking. My Dad's cooking wasn't as good. My clothes dye. My Dad doesn't know how to wash them properly ... this affects the way I look. I don't like to look scruffy."

For a 12 year old boy such simple concerns may seem trivial in relation to the deeper and complex emotional results of a parental break up that we as professionals can identify. Yet clearly, 'looking scruffy' can be of enormous importance within the social life of the school and the essential acceptance by the powerful, and threatening peer culture as illustrated in the previous section.

For another pupil the divorce of his parents was perceived as a release of tension and unhappiness within the house, and conflict that the pupil had been experiencing was dissipated. As Ivan cheerfully stated:

> "My Mum and Dad got divorced in the end. I was happy about that."

Dave offered an interesting insight into the way that a professional opinion can differ from the pupils' own perspective. Concerning his parents divorce he explained:

Divorce

Certain pupils blame parental separation for their difficulties.

Some pupils view the separation of their parents as a positive event alleviating certain problems at home.

Parental separation may not be as significant for some children as professionals believe.

"My Mum and Dad, they're divorced, and they said, it's all to do with that. It's not, because I still see my real Dad everyday. I call my step dad 'Dad'. They just use that as an excuse."

Family relationships and role models

Six pupils described conflict with one particular parent or step-parent that had caused problems for them in their home. Jeremy described his relationship with his mother:

"Mum used to whack me, the only thing she used to do was whack me constantly. She's a bitch."

Another pupil described his relationship with his mother:

"She was always annoying me cause we never got on."

Other pupils, Neil, Karl, Ivan and Karen had negative relationships with their fathers or step-fathers. Some of their comments were:

"I'm always having arguments with my Dad. My Dad got me in the shower and went to punch me."

"I can always remember my Dad beating me up, just because he thought I weren't his kid. I don't look like him."

"I don't think I hate anyone that much except for one person ... my Dad."

This last comment from Karen was supported with further comments about her father including accounts of physical violence:

Aggression at Home

"It was bruises and black eyes."

Some pupils describe parents arguing and fighting at home.

She described her feelings as:

"Every time I see my Dad I throw up. I get shaky and hot. I have trouble hearing his voice. I have trouble being in the same house as him."

She described having no-one to talk to and not wanting to be at home or at school:

"I had no-one to talk to about it ... I didn't wanna go to school, but when I was at school I didn't wanna go home ... my Mum wasn't going to say anything against my Dad."

She continued:

"My Mum would lie about it to protect my Dad about what was going on at home."

Interestingly it was not always physically violent relationships with one or more parent that pupils found destructive emotionally and influential to their behaviour. Some pupils made comments that reflected how parents could readily lower their self-esteem and affect their self-image:

> "Dad sometimes puts me down. Calls me thick and stuff."

> "My Dad used to call me stupid."

Danny was very specific about the affect his father's behaviour had on his own moods:

> "Really it's my Dad's fault for annoying me. He annoys me which puts me in a bad mood before I even come to school in the morning. He hits me, calls me names, it don't hurt, it's only mucking about, but if I'm trying to watch TV or play on the computer - he just turns it off. When my friends are round he turns the electric off."

In fact Danny explained how it had been his father hitting a teacher that resulted in him being expelled from school:

> "A teacher hit me and me Dad went up there and hit the teacher."

This parental behaviour and comments such as that made by Rick below concerning the advice given to him by his father, give insight into the important and powerful role models parenting can provide, and the way conflicting messages and values confront pupils:

> "I learnt to bully. I stood up for myself. My Dad told me to, he said you've gotta hit 'em back."

It would seem that inappropriate adult role models and guidance could be quite influential on the behaviour of certain pupils. This is in agreement with the work of Mooney et al (1991) who found that some of the pupils in their study gave the impression that; '...retaliation was legitimate and, in some cases, suggested or sanctioned by parents.' (p111). Some pupils in their study felt 'justified to fight' (p109), even as the initiators of the aggression.

The influence of parental behaviour was particularly significant for Danny who described how he left home very early in the morning, and hung around with his friends in the bus shelter, in order to avoid his Dad, returning home only when he hoped his Dad would be in bed asleep. He also described how this arrangement had resulted in delinquency and his involvement with the police in the local area.

Karen experienced conflict between her parents that she perceived as directly affecting her:

> "There was a lot of pressure at home and my parents were arguing all the time, and taking it out on me."

Negative Attitudes from Parents

Some parents may put down their children.

Inappropriate Adult Role Models

Parents may encourage, legitimise or model inappropriate behaviour.

Parental Conflict

Witnessing conflict between parents in the home may influence a child's behaviour in school.

She also felt pressured by her parents:

> "The pressure of telling me what to do all the time, like do this and do that."

Only one pupil discussed or raised the issue of sexual abuse within the family during the interviewing. Roy described his experiences:

> "And then everything happened with Dad, when I was at X school, and everything went down hill again. I was beginning to get a little better and then my Dad left. I visited him in prison. I felt I had to. I don't think that helped."

Roy became a school refuser, and explained this in terms of his relationship with his mother:

Caring for a Parent

Pupils may refuse school as a result of wanting to care for a parent at home.

> "I didn't want to leave Mum ... that's why I didn't go out much. I didn't like leaving the house."

Simon's description of losing both his parents was a further example of how problems relating to a pupil's family could be perceived as contributing to behavioural difficulties:

> "My Dad died early in my life when I was five and that never really hit me until my Mum died in 1990, then I suddenly realised, I ain't got no parents here."

Simon believed these losses to have had a considerable affect on his own behaviour, yet admitted that he had only recently realised this. As a young boy he had been in a lot of trouble and his behaviour was very disturbing, but he described not knowing why at that time. However, when interviewed he readily linked his behaviour to these events. When asked what he felt were the most important factors contributing to his behaviour he replied:

Death of Parents

A child's behaviour may be influenced significantly by the death of a parent.

> "The break-up of my life really, my parents dying, getting into trouble with the police, going to prison ..."

He described his life as changing dramatically when his mother died and continued:

> "I never used to drink before. I started going out getting drunk at night, hanging around in a group, getting arrested, robbing people, beating up people, nicking cars. Then I started getting kicked out of foster homes, kicked out of children's homes. I ended up in prison. Prison calmed me down a lot."

Looking into the past and linking family events or experiences with behaviour was not something many pupils were able to do. However, two boys at Southdown School did recall early events in their childhood, although it was unclear to what extent they were actually their own memories and feelings or issues that had been discussed and analysed during counselling. Michael recalled:

"My Mum and Dad split up apparently, and my Dad didn't really look after me and neither did my Mum, so they put me in care."

It is not clear to what extent Michael associated recollections of family break up and difficulties with school problems. Although he raised these issues as being important to him, he also made numerous statements regarding the school itself and its role in his difficulties.

Neil similarly recounted his family problems from an early age:

"I've been screwed up quite a lot during my life with problems, family problems from the day I was born. Since there was always rows when I was a baby, with Mike and my Mum. Then they split up and we were on our own."

These pupils obviously perceived such experiences as being important to them and their behaviour, but were not able to expand to any extent as to how or why such experiences affected them.

Siblings

Montgomery (1989) lists potential factors within the social or family background of children which may in some way contribute to a display of disruptive behaviours in school. One factor described is that of a family in which certain siblings are shown favouritism above others, an aspect of family life that was described as significant by a small number of boys at Southdown. Danny expressed feelings of injustice within his family, where a younger sibling was perceived as receiving preferential treatment. He angrily explained:

"The other thing that annoys me is my sister, spoilt little brat, whatever she wants she has to get it."

Danny revealed a deep dislike of his father, which has been previously described. He clearly placed the 'blame' for his problems on his father. Quite perceptively he related his treatment and the unfairness in his family to the fact that he believed his own father was spoilt when a child and was himself the youngest sibling in the family. Ivan also perceived unfair treatment within his home:

"I had to sit there and say to him 'Dad, Dad, Dad', about twenty times, but if my sister went up to him, and said 'Dad', it would be straight away, 'yeh what do you want?'"

Sam was a 15 year old boy at Southdown School, who had been removed from mainstream as a result of social problems with peers and truancy. He described feeling victimised by his siblings. He explained:

"They're nasty to me too. They try to get me into trouble. Something gets broken they tell my Dad it was me."

Similar problems were expressed by Ken:

Recalling Past Events

The ability of children to recall and associate past events with their current actions may be difficult.

93

"I get told off at home, even if it's not my fault."

Clearly these are problems that many young people experience, yet for these particular pupils with EBD they were perceived as significant issues contributing in some way to their overall behaviour patterns. Jeremy described how he perceived his sister to have received favouritism within his family, and reveals how his placement in the special school had affected his own self-concept:

Favouritism

Perceiving unequal or unjust treatment of siblings by parents can be important to certain children.

"My sister is Mummy's little girl, never had to put up with anything. I'm Mummy's little shit face, the one who's in a mental school."

Clearly Jeremy's own personal perspective of himself and the attitude of his family had affected him, and his placement at a special school appears to have contributed to that negative perception.

Gerry also gave an illustration of the importance of competitiveness within the family and particularly sibling relationships in contributing to the difficulties that can be experienced by pupils with EBD. He was a twin, and while his brother had been able to continue in a mainstream school, Gerry had not because of his learning difficulties and behaviour:

"I was jealous of my brother as well, because he was at a different school to me and he was with all my mates and his mates and we always hang around together, and that really did split us up."

In addition, Gerry had an elder brother who had been sent to a residential EBD school. He perceived his parents as wanting to do the same with him:

"They liked the idea of sending me away to a boarding school because I weren't getting on at home. They'd done it with my brother John."

It would seem that Gerry had a complex combination of family and school problems to deal with:

"I got suspended for smoking in the school bogs. I didn't care what Mum and Dad thought of me. My Dad used to call me stupid when I got suspended. I used to have fights with them, he used to say you'll get put in a home."

Gerry simply perceived his home-life as unjust. He repeatedly complained of being grounded for his behaviour when his twin brother was not. Karen also added significant comments concerning sibling rivalry and parental pressure to succeed:

"A lot of pressure from my Mum to do good."

She added:

"I was always being told I should be more like my brother."

She also described a feeling of injustice, of being blamed for things happening in the family, particularly emotional events:

> "Anytime anything goes wrong it's my fault."

> "If someone's upset, I did it."

Two other pupils also mentioned older siblings as having influenced their behaviour. William at Southdown claimed that his reason for being at that school was:

> "I wanted to follow in my brothers footsteps."

Johnny described smoking as a specific activity, unacceptable to his parents and school that his older brother encouraged him to do:

> "He's the one who got me to smoke, 'cause he is my brother ... I thought to smoke was good, to be like the same as him."

Family and school

It was difficult for some pupils to know where their problems originated, and they were unclear whether problems in the home had created school problems or vice versa. Karl stated:

> "It did affect my home life, so I was always getting in fights at home."

However, he did also state the opposite:

> "Things that happen at home affect the way I am at school I think."

Ken stated:

> "Because of problems at school, it led on to start them at home."

He described initial support from his family following problems in school, but then the frustration of his parents. He perceived injustice and lack of support:

> "At first they were helpful, then they started to get annoyed with me, when I kept coming home, they started shouting at me. Then I get sent to my room anytime anything happened. It's still a bit like that now. I get told off at home, go to my room, even if it's not my fault."

Two pupils interestingly admitted to bringing difficulties at school back into the home. Their personal experiences of bullying at school manifested themselves in the home in the form of bullying of family members or friends. Karl recalled:

> "When I get home I bully people at home ... I didn't use to do it, but since I've been bullied I do it to other people now ... my brother, brother's friends. It doesn't make me feel better."

Jealousy And Competition

Sibling rivalry may influence behaviour.

95

Problems in Different Settings

Problem behaviours in one environment may lead to problems elsewhere.

Karen also admitted to behaviour at home of which she was not proud, following her own experiences of being victimised in school:

> "I'd come home and thump my sister, and I'd feel really bad. I tried to explain to her the way it is, I didn't really mean it, but she just ignores me. I used to just pick a fight with her over nothing. I can see that now. It's kinda the same sort of thing, isn't it? Like if you're having a hard time you're gonna take it out on someone else. It's like I wasn't gonna go up to the bullies and thump them one was I? I was gonna take it out on someone defenceless."

These statements illustrate the way in which the different social systems making up a pupil's life interact, and how problems within one system often create problems within another. Finding the root of the problem, in the family, in school, in the self, is then a very complex issue.

Taking the Blame

Children may perceive their own behaviours as creating serious problems between their parents.

Finally it is important to recognise that some pupils with EBD may feel that they hold responsibility for events within their families. Such pupils can perceive that their own problems create other problems for their family members. For example Karl took the blame for parental disharmony in his family.

> "I was always making my Mum and Dad argue."

Susan, in an informal interview which was untaped, perceived that her problems within school, which largely consisted of panic attacks and running away, had created such tension within the home that her step father had as a result committed suicide.

Family and bullying

In contrast to those pupils who felt that their own difficulties had created problems within the family, others perceived their families as having created problems for them. As previously discussed, becoming a victim to bullying in the school setting may be related to many factors, but for two of the pupils interviewed the reasons were clear. Wayne seemed totally ashamed of not only his parents' age, but also their appearance and economic status:

> "It was my parents fault ... too old, too poor, wear awful clothes."

His own father appeared to have reinforced Wayne's beliefs:

> "Dad says don't have kids when you're that age. He reckons that's been half the problem."

Johnny had experienced similar problems. He perceived his father as not fitting the socially acceptable norm and described this as resulting in teasing.

> "My Dad was too old for my Mum."

For both boys this provocation had resulted in them retaliating and defending their family members. John also experienced a similar need to defend his family:

"I'd lose my rag when people say things about my family."

Dave also made this very clear:

"I thumped him because he called my Mum a name which nearly everyone in school would have done. I don't care if they're twice the size of me, or if I win or lose."

Support

Where relationships within the immediate family were problematical, a small number of pupils described supportive relationships with extended family members as being important to them. A grandparent, uncle or aunt, were mentioned as offering refuge or support from stress within the home. Danny, who has previously been introduced as having problems relating to his father, described the support of other family members:

"I always have dinner at my Nan's and go on holiday with my uncle."

Simon explained how he had tried to find respite from home for a few months:

"I tried going to live with my Nan for five months."

Tom and Ivan received material support when the closer family was unwilling or unable to do so:

"My aunt spoils me."

"My Nan helps me out a lot, she buys me things and lets me borrow money."

These supportive relationships with close relatives were clearly of great value to these boys, yet the loss of an important, caring family member was also perceived by a few pupils as having been a trigger for difficulties and problem behaviour. Jeremy described such a loss:

"My Grandad died two years ago. That affected me badly. I was kicked out of school every other week."

Gerry also recalled:

"It was the time my Grandad died, so everything was going cock up then."

Another pupil, Roy, equated school problems with the death of his grandfather:

"Then my Grandad died. Things just got worse and worse."

Bullying and Parents

Pupils describe being bullied as a result of their parents being of low economic status, being older than average or having an unusual appearance.

Support from Relatives

Children may value relationships with close relatives when family problems persist.

Loss of a close relative may contribute to or escalate problems.

Pupils as carers

A small number of the pupils interviewed had been able to analyse their experiences at home sufficiently well to perceive themselves as carers, which in certain cases had created problems for them. Sarah analysed her own problems as follows:

> "My Mum says I'm 13 going on 18. That's the way I've been brought up, in the pub. I do sometimes feel I've got to take control of Mum, like when she's ill. I took control of the house really, that made me grow up a lot. I think that's why I can't socialise with people my own age, 'cause I find them too immature. I find it easier mixing with people like Karen."

The roles and responsibilities of a child in the home, particularly as carers for other family members, is something that must be taken seriously by those working to support pupils with behaviour difficulties. Fox (1995) discusses absenteeism from school related to anxiety about parents or other home based factors and introduces the idea of CHR, or children with home responsibilities. (p222). Roy provides an interesting example of such a child. As previously described his father was found to have been abusing his sisters and he described how his sense of responsibility for his mother and sisters had affected his behaviour:

Children as Carers

Children may adopt caring roles within the family that impact on their behaviour.

> "I think I didn't want to leave my Mum, like when I first went to school, she was in hospital. That's why I didn't go out much, I didn't like leaving the house ...I was confused ...I worried about my Mum. Everything added together. I had all the trouble at X High School."

This may support Montgomery (1989) who considers '...fear of separation from mother as a key issue' in school refusal (p50). The pupils' perceptions indicate how important it is for professionals to be aware of the responsibilities that their home lives may thrust upon them, and to accommodate these emotional ties that children may have. It is very important as Fox (1995) suggests that we do not allow schools to become detached from the communities they serve.

Social class and socioeconomic status

Interestingly, despite much research linking low social and economic status to disruptive behaviour, only a minority of the pupils associated these factors with behavioural difficulties. These pupils perceived that their acceptance from their peer group was affected, a point that was developed previously. Wayne was clear in his perception of why he had been a victim of bullying in school, associating it directly with his family's social class:

> "It's usually background ... being different to all of them. I lived in a council estate, and that was it ... I was less well off. Dad lost his job, his finances went down. That affected me quite a lot. I was less fortunate."

98

It was of course unlikely that Wayne's family were the only ones living under such conditions, yet in his eyes it clearly created a rift between him and other children. Ivan also perceived a lack of money within his family as affecting his own image:

> "But I wish I had another Dad kinda thing. I can't stand living on income support with my Mum cause I don't have any clothes."

It is interesting and important to note how the pupils' fear of deviating from the peer group norms can be so closely related to socioeconomic status, illustrating how important 'being different' can be for certain pupils. George bluntly described lack of money and food as the motives for his aggressive behaviour at school:

> "We didn't get much pocket money then ... we was hungry. I was always hungry."

> "We'd nick people's dinner money."

If George's statements are accurate then clearly this is evidence that a simple link may exist in certain cases between poverty and unacceptable behaviour, although to separate this from self-image and self-esteem issues may be an over simplification.

A small number of pupils were able to look beyond immediate family, and described their broader social environment as having influenced their behaviour. Simon stated:

> "It's just my background, the way I was brought up. I mean, I was bullied into petrol bombing in the stadiums, breaking into people's homes."

He explained his behaviour:

> " ... because of where I lived and the people I mixed with."

Simon certainly appeared to be linking the violence and criminality in his immediate social environment to his own problems. George also perceived his difficulties to have been compounded by the area in which his family lived. Problems involving neighbouring families had resulted in George being threatened and having to live in a Children's Home:

> "I had to come out [of school] cause of some trouble down my road, then I was put in care. I wasn't allowed in the area. The area we came from it's really rough."

Alan was a 14 year old boy attending the Oakwood Centre. He had been expelled from previous mainstream schools as result of disruptive behaviours and had also been in trouble out of school. He described teasing and bullying that resulted from his family and their lifestyle. In particular he was considered a gypsy by school peers:

Self Image

Low social or economic status may be perceived by a child as a critical obstruction to their acceptance by peers and may also affect their self image.

Poverty

Certain pupils recognise that poverty may be a motive for their behaviours.

Cultural Expectations

Some delinquent behaviours are simply the norm in certain environments.

Unacceptable Cultural Groups

Certain children are rejected by their peers on the basis of their cultural identity, including travellers.

99

"They called me Pikey."

He also described how his mother couldn't afford to send him to a good school in the district:

"My Mum couldn't afford to pay for all the things that school asked for."

Such statements clearly illustrate the potential impact of a pupil's socioeconomic and cultural status on their behaviour.

Conflicting goals and values

A minority of pupils did hint at a mismatch between the goals of their schooling and their wider social and cultural values. However, in some cases the pupils expressed positive thoughts regarding the value of schooling and regrets as to their lack of success within the system. Surprisingly just one pupil openly expressed a complete rejection of school. This was Ronnie, who considered school unable to provide him with anything of value, preferring to subscribe to the value system of his peer culture out of school, which primarily appeared to revolve around drugs. He explained:

"There hasn't been school ... I couldn't give a shit."

Simon placed his own unique value on the special school he attended:

"I saw coming here as somewhere to doss during the day, so I wasn't stuck at home all the time. I don't really do much work ... I come into school to chill out."

His comment hints at one possible reason why the special school setting may support pupils with EBD in a way that a mainstream school does not. It may be a place offering more than academic opportunity, but also respite from the demands of the pupils' family or social existence. This is in agreement with Cooper (1989,1992) who investigated at length the pupils' perception of their residential special schooling, and who claims that respite is an important aspect of the provision made for them.

Key points emerging from this section

- Years of research and statistical evidence suggest that there are underlying patterns which link social factors to a child's behaviour, although open debate continues regarding these correlations and research continues to attempt to explain how or why these trends exist.

- The pupils' own perceptions suggest that the influence of a pupil's family, socioeconomic and sociocultural background on their behaviour is an important consideration.

- Issues such as divorce of parents, death of family members, abuse or adopting the role of carer in the family may all have an impact on behaviour in school.

The Value of School

Some pupils see no value in school while others have their own unique view of what it can offer them.

- Anything unusual about a parent or coming from a low-income family can affect a child's self image and esteem which in turn can affect behaviour.

- Each individual pupil obviously presents a unique combination of factors, of varying significance, which could be used to explain behaviour. To ignore any possible factors and focus solely on the family and related issues would be to oversimplify the problem.

- Pupils made fewer comments about family and social issues than about schooling factors and in certain cases discussing these aspects of their lives resulted in distress.

- A true assessment of the relative importance of social and family factors in influencing behaviour in relation to other factors is difficult to make.

Thoughts for your reflection

- When working with children with EBD to what extent do you believe it is valuable to be aware of their family backgrounds and social/economic status?

- Do you actively seek to explore factors existing beyond the school when trying to better understand the behaviour of challenging students?

- Do you think that academic and behavioural expectations in the classroom should change if you become aware of difficulties that a child is experiencing outside school?

- How do you respond if a pupil describes events or situations outside school that may be influencing their behaviour?

- How committed are you to communicating with parents over difficult behaviour and how effective do you consider your skills to be regarding such communication?

- What are your views on residential schooling for children with EBD that removes them from their home and family?

3.3 Things about me: Physiological and Psychological Factors

This section presents the pupils' perceptions of personal factors, of a physiological or psychological nature, that they considered to have in some way influenced their behaviour. Included in this section are the pupils' perceptions of therapeutic treatment and its affect on their behaviour.

As noted earlier, in attempting to make sense of human behaviour, particularly that of an anti-social nature, many theorists and researchers have considered contributing factors or problems as lying within the individual. They have viewed the person themselves as being an important component of the problem, if not the problem. In other words, certain physical and psychological

Understanding Behaviour

Medical, developmental, emotional and genetic factors may all influence behaviour.

101

variables may predispose them to behave in a deviant fashion, regardless of their social experiences. Such internal factors may be of a purely biological or medical nature, an example being that described in an early study (Graham & Rutter, 1968) showing that 34% of epileptic children had behaviour problems. Problems may also be seen to be of a psychodynamic nature, that is, based on the quality of early relationships, or of a psychomedical nature, resulting from disturbed developmental processes. According to those who support such theories of behaviour, both of these could potentially lead to unconscious emotions and conflicts, or abnormal personalities. There are also possible psychometric factors that are seen to contribute in some way to low intellectual functioning and subsequently to some behavioural problems. In terms of genetic foundations for behaviour, researchers attempting to link disturbed behaviour to genetic roots using twins, have yet to produce evidence that confidently confirms a link between genetic make-up and a predisposition to behaviour problems. (Scherer et al, 1990).

Research Evidence

There are problems relating biological factors to disturbing behaviour and the nature/nurture debate continues.

The extent to which such factors are responsible for the behaviour of pupils with EBD is an issue of ongoing debate. Perhaps the reason for this is that so little concrete evidence exists to verify the presence of such factors. Charlton & David (1989) consider that little research has been carried out into the biological factors associated with disturbed behaviour and they propose that any such factors that do manifest themselves in behaviour are hard to analyse. They suggest that the factors that have been most researched are the psychodynamic factors, such as the influence of family experiences and relationships during the early years of development. Such factors are thought to manifest themselves subconsciously in behaviour. Research into deviant or 'extreme' personalities also continues but remains somewhat inconclusive. (Fontana, 1986). In summary, it is clearly difficult to totally separate a psychologically or biologically based reason for behaviour from possible social influences.

Medical Diagnosis

ADD continues as a controversial yet common label for challenging children both in the UK and he USA.

Medical models for behaviour and associated treatments may conflict with and inhibit social analysis of problem behaviour

However, despite the lack of solid research evidence many professionals have readily adopted the concept of a biologically or psychologically based disorder from which to 'treat' the child with EBD. Scherer et al (1990) though aware that such traditional approaches tend to ignore the social context of behaviour and over estimate the consistency of certain behaviours in different situations, do suggest that to ignore them completely could be wrong. They describe evidence of some cross-situational consistency in behaviour and also of disruptive behaviour having been shown to be related to individual and background characteristics. Galloway & Goodwin (1987) similarly state that 'we should not, however, overlook the possibility that physical factors may also play a part.' (p47). Even relatively recently a psychiatric diagnosis for difficult children has established itself in this country called Attention Deficit Hyperactivity Disorder (ADHD), or Attention Deficit Disorder (ADD) (Cooper, 1994, Hinshaw, 1994, Prior, 1997). This disorder covers a wide range of symptoms including the behaviour of disturbing and challenging children, and that of children who have difficulty concentrating, processing or retaining information. Research reveals that there is some concrete medical evidence of such a syndrome existing. However, there are strong concerns as to the extent to which it is becoming a convenient label for certain pupils that can be used to explain away a number of behaviours which could otherwise be considered from a non-medical perspective. Drugs are generally used to treat the syndrome and with an estimated four million children in the USA being diagnosed as sufferers and being administered drugs this has lead to serious ethical questions. Ideus (1994) traces the development of the disorder back to the 1970's and 1980's in the USA. and she believes that the Americans are conditioned to accept the authority of the medical profession on issues such as ADHD, and therefore have not been prepared to accept or investigate a sociological analysis of the problem. However, much research continues on ADHD, and the advocates of the various theoretical models of behaviour continue to interpret it within their own belief structures.

The tendency to use a medical model for explaining disruptive or disturbing behaviour of children in schools is not new. Dyslexia, although more associated with learning difficulties, could be considered another example of a frequently used and possibly abused term offering what many consider to be a convenient explanation for certain children's inadequacies. It is interesting that we continue to pursue tangible explanations for disturbing behaviours offered by the medical profession, in order to find a means of controlling it. Ideus (1994) suggests that this reflects the unwillingness of our society to accept that cultural factors may play an important role in deviant behaviour. The convenience of a medical label far outweighs any desire to seek out answers that may reveal or lie within the weakness of society and its values. Corbett & Norwich (1997) link medical labelling of difficult children to political forces and a need to obtain certain resources. They also see parents as exploiting certain special needs diagnoses, presumably of a medical nature, to gain privileged services for their children.

Medical Labels

Use of medical labelling may mask the impact of other systemic problems and may be exploited to control behaviour through the use of drugs by focusing on the child alone.

The study on which this book is based set out to explore the extent to which the pupils themselves perceive their behavioural problems to be a result of their own physiological or psychological malfunctioning. It seemed important to explore whether society's tendency to use medical terminology and labelling of disturbing behaviour had influenced pupils' perceptions of themselves, and as a result the level of personal responsibility they accept for their behaviour. The results illustrate the nature and extent of the pupils' perceptions of themselves as contributing factors influencing their difficulties, and the extent to which they believe their own bodies, minds, personalities or temperaments should be seen to influence their behaviour.

Pupils' Perceptions

Little research has sought to reveal the extent to which children view their own physiological or psychological make-up as influencing their behavioural problems.

Pupils' perception of themselves

Some pupils perceived a simple physical trait as influencing their social interaction with other pupils, creating social pressures and therefore indirectly influencing their behaviours. As previously discussed, any physical deviance from the socially accepted norms of their peer group has the potential to create stress for certain pupils. Six pupils linked their problems with being bullied to their small physical stature, illustrating how a simple factor like their physical size can greatly influence a pupil's experiences in school. John, perceived another aspect of his appearance to be related to his problems:

"I'm small, fat, ugly."

As previously described, pupils also considered their clothes and hair in addition to their own bodies as crucial to their social status and acceptance. Karen commented:

> "If you haven't got much money and if you haven't got the right clothes and shoes, or don't have your hair done the right way, it's like you're different."

Being Different

Some children appear to be conscious of any aspect of their appearance that makes them different.

Any differences can trigger problems for a child.

Social or economic status may alienate a child.

Seeking individuality may be difficult for pupils in school.

As Karen's comment reveals, although these factors relate to money and the socioeconomic status of the family, they become a part of the individual's personal difficulties in school. Karen also offered a different perspective regarding how problems with peers may arise:

> "Also when you go through puberty, you start developing before other people."

Sarah described other physical factors that she believed had enhanced her feelings of being different:

> "I was the first person with glasses... first person with braces."

Three pupils also perceived themselves as different to others in terms of their attitudes. Sam stated:

> "I'm different to the others, different points of view and stuff."

Karen also added comments regarding her attitude:

> "I was kind of different. I didn't like playing the games they were playing, doing the things they were doing. I didn't join in much."

These feelings were also described by Mike, who stated:

> "I couldn't communicate with people my own age."

For these pupils their own individuality had put them at risk of losing acceptance by their peer group, and as Karen stated:

> "If you weren't in a group, you weren't worth talking to."

Those pupils who had experienced academic difficulties within the mainstream school setting were often quick to blame the system, that is the teachers and the curriculum, as shown in previous sections. However, there were a small number of pupils who perceived themselves as being responsible for their inability to manage class work and meet academic expectations. They were readily prepared to locate the problem within themselves. Four pupils commented:

> "It's only my fault for not understanding."

> "I can't write properly. I can't read properly."

"I didn't know how to read. I didn't know how to do anything then."

"I don't know much. I'm thick."

Karen considered that her problems had been created by a combination of her own inadequacies coupled with the school itself:

"It wasn't just the school it was me as well."

"It wouldn't have been the school's fault if I'd stick up for myself."

She tried to define her problem in terms of exactly which aspect of the school had highlighted her own inadequacies:

"It wasn't actually the school, it was only the people."

Two pupils felt that their behaviour had been within their own control and hence took responsibility for subsequent problems. Rick stated:

"I blame myself. If I'd behaved and hadn't messed about all the time, I wouldn't be here now, would I ?"

Certain pupils did not hesitate to lay the reasons for their behaviour squarely on the shoulders of certain uncontrollable personality traits. Bobby described himself as 'disruptive' and stated:

"It's out of my control sometimes."

Temper was one of the most frequently described reasons for behaviour:

"I couldn't control my temper."

"I lose my temper easily."

"My temper's hard to control."

"I had a shorter fuse than anyone else."

John stated that if he could change anything:

" I'd change my temper if I could. Once I lose my rag, I lose my rag."

These pupils, interestingly all boys, appeared to perceive being controlled by their tempers. Another pupil described having no control over his behaviour at all, stating:

"I couldn't help being naughty."

Blaming Yourself

Some pupils readily blame their physical appearance or their personalities for their behaviours.

The impact of support and treatment on pupils' perceptions of themselves

Many of the pupils who were interviewed had received or were receiving treatment or support from a range of professionals including psychiatrists. Possibly as a result, some of them described their difficulties using medical vocabulary and terminology. Slee (1994) refers to the work of Armstrong et al (1993) who suggest '...the students come to see themselves in terms of the medical discourse.' (p159). For example pupils used words such as phobia, paranoia, claustrophobia and agoraphobia when describing themselves. Sarah was quite clear in her perception of what her own problem was:

"I've got a school phobia."

Karen similarly had labels for her difficulties:

"Being on your own in a large space, agoraphobia, that's always been a part of me. The claustrophobic part came when I was at school 'cause there was so many people."

In a later interview she also described her fear of school and bullying as paranoia:

"I built up this thing in my mind that I knew it was going to happen, so I couldn't go. Being more paranoid than it actually happening ... I was getting really paranoid. I couldn't walk down the street without looking behind me."

Other comments also suggest that labels given to pupils can strongly influence the way in which they perceive themselves:

"I've got attitude problems."

"I've got an addictive personality, it gets carried down through the genes."

Labelling a child can create a perception that any problems lie firmly within that individual. This angers certain professionals who believe that this simply relieves the need to seek answers within a wider social context, and offers greater and more powerful opportunities for controlling deviancy. However, some of the pupils' comments suggested a sense of relief at having a medical term equated with their behaviour. Sarah welcomed the opportunity to become a psychiatric patient following her refusal to attend a mainstream school and a suicide attempt:

"I liked people saying I was getting psychiatric help ... I wanted everyone to know I had a problem ... Being in a psychiatric hospital told everyone I had a problem."

It appears that the psychiatric treatment gave validity and credibility to her problem. She continued:

"I wanted to shout to everyone 'God help me', and the only way I could do that was to be in a psychiatric unit."

Clearly, being labelled as disordered or 'sick' may remove responsibility for behaviour from the individual. In fact it may remove responsibility from everyone apart from the 'experts', as Slee (1994) suggests; 'Responsibility becomes the privilege and prerogative of the 'expert'.' (p159). For this reason Slee also suggests that parents may welcome such labelling and treatment. He suggests that if they are '...used to having their child seen as bad, the status of 'impaired' is frequently preferred.' (p159).

Not all pupils agreed with Sarah however. Some appeared more angered by the suggestion that they 'had a problem' and needed help. For example Jeremy, who perceived tension within the family and his relationship with his mother as being a major reason for his behaviour, certainly did not welcome the suggestion that he himself may be the problem, and that he have psychiatric treatment to 'cure' that problem:

"I went to this crappy thing ... all I used to do was beat the living daylights out of a punching bag and that was it. Lock me in a room ... I didn't see the point of it, supposed to be stress relief. As if I was under stress!"

Jeremy continued by saying:

"When I had to talk it lasted for about three hours. It really got to me."

The decision to provide treatment clearly frustrated and confused a number of pupils. Susan had been attending the Oakwood Centre as a result of admission to a psychiatric unit. Her perceptions of herself were obviously different from those of the professionals who had diagnosed and referred her:

"Maybe I have got problems, but I haven't known any anyway."

Two other pupils believed that they were in control of their own thoughts and behaviour and any attempts to change them were futile:

"What was going on in my mind was going on in my mind. No one could change that. No one could change the way I was feeling."

"It's up to me, just me. I'll change sooner or later."

Roy explained the pressure that seeing a psychiatrist placed on him:

"And I was under pressure at the time to find out what was wrong."

Armstrong et al (1993) suggest that pupils receiving treatment lack information about the purposes and outcomes of psychological and medical interviews. Roy reinforced this view when he stated:

Labelling Behaviour

Professionals often seek to label behaviours.

Certain pupils readily use given labels when describing themselves and their behaviours.

Labels appear to be welcomed by some pupils.

Labels may serve to shift the responsibility for behaviour from one person to another.

"It was quite confusing really. I didn't know who my doctor was, or who I was supposed to talk to."

In general, the majority of pupils who described psychiatric treatment in their interviews were negative about the process and its success. Roy had been a school refuser and as a result was admitted to a residential psychiatric treatment unit as an alternative to a boarding school. Fearing that the boarding school option would do little to alleviate his problems, he had elected to try treatment. His perception of this treatment was:

"The Unit didn't help at all ... made me more angry ... no it didn't do nothing for me at all."

Karen also expressed negative perceptions of the value of psychiatric treatment in helping with school problems:

"I don't know why I was in there."

Following her period in the psychiatric unit she unhesitatingly stated:

"Problems with school, I don't think psychiatrists can help at all."

She added:

"I think being in [the psychiatric unit] was a waste of time ...The only therapy we had was large group therapy and art therapy, that was a waste of time anyway. If no one wanted to speak no one spoke. If you didn't wanna answer anyone's questions you didn't have to. And you didn't actually talk about what was going on, or how you needed help. Basically the anorexics they could feed them and the depressed they could put on medications."

Two other boys at Southdown had similar perceptions. Bobby summed up his experience of psychiatrists:

"That's all they do, sit and talk to you. No if you ask me they don't do any good at all. They just sit there and ignore ya."

Simon, who had seen a number of different psychiatrists and other professionals for his violent and delinquent behaviour, considered none of it to have helped:

"They just sit there and ask deep questions."

Susan also recounted the ineffectiveness of such treatment, combined with feelings of confusion and anxiety. She received psychiatric treatment following recurring panic attacks in school and the suicide of her stepfather:

"Dr J. just talked all the time. He didn't do much. Then they moved me onto this other man, it was hard. He did this relaxation with me and I just pretended I was doing it. I didn't like doing it at all. Couldn't never do it anyway. I don't know why but he used to scare me. They used to say, don't be stupid but when he stood up, breathed in and out it scared me. The more I got to see him, the more he was alright, until he started to do the relaxation thing ... I haven't seen any of them for ages. I don't want to."

Wayne described the stigma of receiving treatment, and a certain amount of fear. He felt that the adolescent unit for treatment should not have been in the middle of a psychiatric hospital.

> "People would go in there and were scared ... it was so bleak, it looked so much like a hospital. It scared the hell out of you ... old geriatrics running around, people that are gone in the head."

For a number of the pupils who dismissed psychiatric treatment as being a waste of time, their perceptions of the value of the small supportive special school was quite the opposite. It would appear that they perceived the school as offering more appropriate and valuable support than a medically or psychologically based treatment programme. Johnny described the Oakwood Centre as important for him because:

> "Here they care."

Such a comment suggests that pupils may recognise the need for specialised support and care but do not necessarily equate this with treatment or therapy.

Key points emerging from this section

- Some of the pupils in this study made comments indicating that they considered themselves or their families as damaged and unacceptable or as deviant in some way.

- Physical deviancy can lead to a problem being accepted by the peer group and subsequent bullying.

- It appears that medical or therapeutic intervention can influence a pupil's perception of themselves and they may use official terminology or labels to describe themselves.

- In some cases therapeutic intervention was perceived as ineffective or damaging.

- Many pupils appeared less inclined to talk of personal factors as contributing to their behaviour than they were to describe schooling factors. To what extent this is a reflection of their own perceptions of the problems, or an indication of their lack of willingness or confidence to talk openly about these issues is unclear.

Thoughts for your reflection

- When you are working with pupils who regularly display challenging or difficult behaviours to what extent do you personally believe there to be a physiological or psychological problem within the child?

The Value of Treatment

Some pupils are dubious about the role of psychiatric treatment in helping their behaviour or problems.

109

- What are your beliefs concerning the use of medical interventions or therapy for children with EBD?

- Are you alert to the way in which a child's perception of him or her self can influence his or her behaviour?

- Are you aware of the way in which children can internalise an official or unofficial label they are given relating to their behaviour and how this may in turn impact their perceptions of themselves and their subsequent actions?

Some final thoughts from chapter 3

- Pupils with EBD perceive a variety of factors and processes as having influenced their behaviour.

- The factors they describe can be placed into the following categories:

  Schools and teachers
  Families and life outside school
  Themselves.

- Factors associated with mainstream schools and teachers received the most criticism and comments from pupils but methodological limitations may have contributed to this result.

- Each pupil is a unique case whose statements illustrate that a complex combination of factors can influence behaviour.

- The complexity of the factors described by the pupils suggest that pupils with EBD may be more vulnerable to failure in school than other children and need more specific support structures in the mainstream setting if they are to succeed in that setting.

- To truly understand and support pupils with EBD it may be necessary to utilise and embrace a variety of theoretical models of behaviour.

4 How we see it:

The children's perceptions of their own behaviours

In this chapter I have focused on the pupils' perceptions of their own behaviour. It is presented in three sections:

4.1 Pupils describe their behaviours and motives.

4.2 How behaviours evolve and are labelled.

4.3 How children look for support and understanding.

Chapter 3 presented factors that were perceived by pupils as having made a significant contribution to the difficulties they had experienced and their behaviour. This chapter attempts to develop a greater understanding of the different behaviours that were displayed by the pupils in this study using pupils' perceptions to describe and categorise them. It also attempts to better understand the meaning of the behaviour as perceived by the pupils themselves, by exploring and presenting pupils' motives for their behaviour. I have looked for patterns in the data which may reflect links between certain behaviours and motives, and the way in which specific behaviours may result from the different factors or experiences presented in the previous chapter. The role of labelling is analysed using the pupils' perspective, and the way in which behaviour patterns evolve and develop is discussed using pupils' accounts of their own case histories. Finally, the pupils' attempts at finding support and understanding are described using their own voices.

4.1 Pupils describe their behaviours and motives

Motive or rationale behind difficult or disruptive behaviour in schools has not always been of interest to researchers. Many have been more concerned with equating behaviour with social or psychological factors as described in previous chapters. Such factors are believed to directly stimulate the individual to behave in a certain way, crediting him or her with little control over his or her actions. This positivist approach has been challenged by interactionist studies that have had quite an impact on educational research and our understanding of difficult children. Interactionist approaches propose that human beings

Theories of Behaviour

Some theories equate behaviour with social or psychological factors.

Educational research has been influenced by theories that believe individuals have control over their own actions.

act towards things on the basis of the meanings that the things have for them and that individuals use an interpretive process to create and modify meaning. Obviously this equates with humans being able to reflect on themselves, and having a degree of control over their behaviours; they make decisions.

Just as theories of behaviour have evolved so has the terminology used to describe different behaviours. Defining and classifying the behaviours of pupils with EBD has been an ongoing problem for many years as behaviour is so open to subjective interpretation. (See chapter 1). To label certain behaviour as 'deviant' or 'disruptive' involves taking into account the context of that behaviour, including the values and attitudes of the observer. Galloway & Goodwin (1987) quote from a report compiled in 1985 for the ILEA that stated; 'Disabilities and difficulties become more or less handicapping depending on the expectations of others and on social contexts.' (p24). It is therefore very difficult to define exactly what constitutes 'problem' behaviour. It is also difficult to find suitable terminology for such behaviour. Words used in the past such as 'handicapped', or 'maladjusted' were established as far back as the 1940's and 1950's in documents such as The Handicapped Pupils and School Health Regulations (DES, 1945) and The Underwood Report (DES, 1955). Other terms have included 'disorder' and 'disturbance', which originated largely amongst the medical personnel who were involved in diagnosis. Such terms certainly suggested that the child required treatment of some sort and seemed to pay little regard to the social context of the behaviour.

Defining Difficult Behaviours

Describing and categorising behaviour can be stigmatising.

Defining terms may affect the number of pupils entitled to special provision.

The Warnock Report (DES, 1978) and the Education Act (DES, 1981) helped to redefine these stigmatising terms, and a broader concept of Special Educational Needs was introduced. The old terms of handicapping conditions were abolished although the term maladjustment was in fact retained despite the fact that its popularity had been fading during the 1970's. New categories were introduced to define learning difficulties as mild, moderate, severe and specific. The large number of pupils with special needs within the system was also recognised with the introduction of these new broader definitions.

Since then the disruptive, disturbed, disturbing, antisocial, or disaffected child has continued to create problems for those concerned with labelling or defining behaviour (Cooper, 1996). The term maladjusted has been replaced by EBD, or pupils with emotional and behavioural difficulties. A formal definition of this term is given in DES Circular 23/89 as cited in Cooper et al (1994); 'Children who set up barriers between themselves and their learning environment through inappropriate, aggressive, bizarre or withdrawn behaviour' and who 'have developed a range of strategies for dealing with day-to-day experiences that are inappropriate and impede normal personal and social development, and make it difficult for them to learn.' (p20).

However, even this now widely accepted term of EBD has been scrutinised and subdivided further in recent reports. Vivian (1994) recalls a DES draft circular (DES, 1988) as identifying two broad categories used to describe the behaviour of pupils with EBD; (i) Withdrawal, neurotic responses, anxiety states, depression and similar manifestations, (ii) Aggression, violence, delinquency, and socially unacceptable conduct. (p218). He also recalls the earlier work of Dawson (1980) who proposed three categories; (i) CD for conduct disordered,

(ii) ED for neurotic or emotionally disturbed, (iii) a mixture of CD and ED. Clarizio (1992) also proposes that two categories are necessary for appropriate schooling and educational placement, doubting that the two are compatible. From his research in the USA he proposes there is a difference between those young people who are socially maladjusted (SM), yet free from emotional disturbance, and those who are seriously emotionally disturbed (SED). A further development of this debate is proposed by Conner (1994), who interestingly suggests that 'a range of conditions' exist, which form part of an 'EBD spectrum.' (p5). His spectrum includes; (i) Nervous disorder, which includes fears, anxieties, phobias, depression, withdrawal, apathy, compulsions and obsessions, (ii) Habit disorders, including, speech, sleep, movement, eating, and psychosomatic disorders, (iii) Behaviour disorders, including school refusal, truancy, temper loss, aggression, attention demanding, (iv) Organic disorder, including physical disorders like epilepsy, diabetes and physical or sensory handicap, (v) Psychotic disorder which includes extremes of behaviour, (vi) Educational disorders, including poor concentration, being unable to stick to task, dyslexia. He also comments on the highly subjective nature of the identification of children with EBD, and how this subjectivity is reflected in the level of tolerance of the person observing the behaviour. With the introduction of LMS, and government pressure on schools to display league tables and truancy statistics, it is suggested that tolerance of certain behaviours has been reduced. Vivian (1994) questions whether a professional diagnosis is affected by changing perceptions of particular behaviours over time, suggesting that a 'desensitising' (p222) of teachers takes place when they work with pupils with EBD each day. Hence, whether a child is diagnosed as a behaviour disorder or an emotional disorder becomes purely subjective.

Clearly, categorising behaviour is no easy task. Terminology continues to change, and statistics remain based largely on subjective analysis. Cooper (1996) certainly reinforces the fact that there remains a need to develop clearer and more precise terminology, stating; 'EBD is not a satisfactory category' and is '...a crude, ill-defined and not very useful descriptor. Current definitions of the terms are vague and undeveloped.' (p147). Scherer et al (1990) cynically urge us to be careful with the words that we use, saying that labelling is alright as long as '...whenever we use words that are relatively meaningless we acknowledge the fact.' (p26). Whatever terminology we use it is important that we are clear why we are using it. As Blyth & Milner (1994) suggest that we may be enhancing the social control functions of education by this obsession with categorisation and labelling, and Schostak (1983) warns that we may even be considering individuality itself as deviancy.

This chapter presents statements made by the pupils regarding their behaviour and their often highly rational comments offer support to interactionist theories. The pupils were in many cases able to describe their own behaviours and the reasons for those behaviours. They also support some of the concerns previously described regarding how categorising behaviour and labelling can create problems in certain instances. Two broad categories of behaviour have been used to facilitate the presentation of the pupils' perceptions; fight and flight. No attempt is made to propose a new means of categorisation, or to suggest that behaviours fit neatly into either of these two categories. They have simply been used in order to present the pupils' behaviours clearly and where

Using the Term EBD

The term EBD is now widely accepted but continues to be scrutinised.

Subjective interpretation of behaviour continues.

Social Control

Labelling and categorising behaviours may enhance social control and undermine individuality.

Fight or Flight

Behavioural responses to stress or fear may be loosely categorised as fight or flight.

possible to link those behaviours to given motives and justifications. Fight and flight are two behavioural strategies which in scientific terms have been proposed as natural responses to stress or fear, (Moskowitz & Orgel, 1969, Lewis & Peterson, 1974), and the majority of pupil behaviours have been loosely allocated to one or other of these categories. In presenting and discussing what the pupils had to say, an attempt has been made to show the extent of the pupils' interpretation of his or her own actions, and wherever possible this is analysed further within a framework of knowledge about the pupils' specific case history. It is hoped that this chapter will provide teachers and other professionals with valuable insight into how and why certain behaviours occur. Such insight may encourage the development and implementation of improved support structures and intervention strategies for difficult children.

4.1 (i) **Flight**

Behaviours which are included under the term flight include those which appeared to be, or were described as being, attempts to withdraw from problems. Pupils who described this type of strategy had often been influenced by many of the factors described in chapter 3, including problems with social interaction such as teasing, and bullying, or problems associated with the academic expectations of the school.

Flight within the school setting

Flight or withdrawal was initially attempted by some of the pupils actually within the school itself. It appears that a minority of pupils, who did not want to break school rules, tried to find ways to survive within the system. This was often the case for those pupils who perceived themselves as experiencing social not academic problems. These pupils sought ways of avoiding peer interaction, taking the limited opportunities offered to them by the highly social nature of the schooling system. 'Joining in' seems to be a standard expectation for pupils within school from an early age, yet such pressure to constantly be part of a group or to identify with group activities may create problems for certain children. Certain pupils recounted their own personal strategies for avoiding peer interaction. Karen described having to be close to teachers:

> "I didn't join in much ...I used to sit with the teachers, cling to them."

Another pupil, Roy, devised his own personal strategy for separating himself from the social pressures of the classroom:

> "I started to tell rubbish jokes, so everybody wanted me to be put on a different table. I worked much better on a table on my own, cause nobody could have a go at me."

These few comments suggest that schools may need to recognise the needs of certain pupils to be able to take 'time out' from the relentless social pressures of the school setting. Legitimate opportunities to escape the social melee should perhaps be provided in order to prevent pupils having to choose unacceptable alternatives such as truancy or running away.

Flight

An attempt to withdraw from problems may be described as a flight response.

Escaping from Social Pressures

Children with EBD may seek ways to avoid social interaction in school.

Non attendance may result from a lack of legitimate ways to isolate from peers within the school.

Running away

For a number of the pupils the lack of legitimate options for escape or respite resulted in behaviours that involved avoiding school completely. Some attempted to minimise conflict with the school by finding ways round the attendance or registration procedures. As Pasternicki et al (1993) found with their study of truants; 'The accuracy in recording and detecting student absences ... proved variable.' (p5). Three of the pupils described their ability to beat the system including Karen who explained how easy it was to register then to leave school:

> "Go out after first register, come back again at dinner, and do the register, then go out again."

For Karen, who was a bright articulate girl, problems had been primarily with her peer group and she had not wanted to miss classes. She described trying to cope with class time but leaving school just prior to periods of the day where social interaction with peers would be inevitable:

> "I'd register then I'd go to half hour lesson, then I'd say 'can I go to the loo, I need my bag?' and so, goodbye."

Sandra described registering in the morning then leaving for the rest of the day, which was her way of dealing with her academic difficulties:

> "Go to register in the morning then in the afternoon they'd think I was just late, cause I went home to lunch. I missed register nobody said anything."

Alan also found a loophole in the system that allowed him to deal with his social and academic problems:

> "Some days I went, then left after lunch."

When interpreting these comments in relation to the pupils' perceptions of their problems as a whole, it seems that such withdrawal behaviours are quite rational responses to stressful situations. These pupils appeared to lack alternative legitimate behavioural options for dealing with their difficulties or fears.

Another, perhaps spontaneous option for dealing with school problems was to literally run away from the pressures. Sam described his behaviour in response to peer pressure and bullying:

> "I ran home. They stopped me from doing my work so I had to make it up during PE and everyone started laughing at me, so I just got right on my bike and went home."

Mike explained his response to bullying:

> "I used to run away a lot of the time ... sometimes I used to run away during play times."

Sneaking Out

Some pupils describe leaving school after registering attendance. This may be a way to avoid academic or social difficulties.

Susan also ran away from peer pressure. She perceived her only other options as being aggressive or seeking support, both of which she rejected:

> "And I did get wound up and ever since that happened I couldn't handle it any more, so instead of turning round and hitting them, and I couldn't tell the teachers cause they don't do anything, I ran out."

This statement illustrates the three behaviour options a pupil may face when experiencing difficulties: fight, flight or find support. In this case Susan described flight as her chosen action. Mike was also aware that flight was preferable to a more violent alternative:

> "I lost my temper, I got fed up, and I didn't want to come to school."

He explained why he ran away:

> "Because I was threatening people, I was losing my temper because of those boys bullying me."

Gerry was able to explain how being denied one form of 'escape' from his problem simply resulted in an alternative having to be found. He described how his learning difficulties had embarrassed and frustrated him, resulting in him truanting from school. When an attempt was made to extinguish this unacceptable behaviour by placing Gerry in a boarding school, he simply resorted to running away:

Running Away

Feeling angry, embarrassed or humiliated can create the need to run away from school.

> ".... because of that school, I couldn't bunk off, so that was a problem ... I used to run away."

For Gerry it would appear that the real problem was not being addressed. Instead his behavioural options for dealing with the problem were being limited without meeting his needs. He was aware of the fact that he was caught in a 'no win' situation, whereby every behavioural option for him created more problems. A vicious circle:

> " ... to cope with a problem I used to run away from it, instead of getting in trouble, but I got in trouble for that as well."

Clearly flight did not provide any long term solutions for these pupils and the feeling of frustration that Gerry described was evident in many of the pupils' accounts of their behaviour and problems. Johnny chose to run away from school when conflict with teachers in the classroom arose. If the teacher's efforts to support him in the classroom did not meet his perceived needs, then Johnny withdrew. He described consciously choosing withdrawal as opposed to a more aggressive response under these circumstances:

> "Cause I didn't know what to do, so I left it there, and she told me to do it and I didn't know what to do. She'd shout at me and I'd get up tight and then I'd run out of school. I don't like people shouting at me. If they get up tight I start shouting at them."

Other statements he made revealed that Johnny's classroom difficulties were rooted in academic difficulties. He described his feeling as 'getting up tight' when he did not get enough support, which could equate to a number of different things including anger, frustration, embarrassment, humiliation or fear. His description seems to suggest that running away was the only way to avoid fighting or shouting. Guy, also a low ability pupil who had academic problems, described his flight response:

> "I kept walking out the classroom. I went home once ..."

He was able to link his academic problems to teasing and peer conflict, illustrating how closely academic and social pressures can be connected:

> "People calling me names and that, and I couldn't take it so I walked home .... They kept calling me names cause I don't know much ..."

In summary, it would appear that running away was a behavioural choice made by pupils to escape from difficult situations and used as a preferable alternative to more aggressive, antisocial options. It was chosen as a solution to problems of both a social and an academic nature.

Refusing to attend and truancy

An extension of these withdrawal or flight behaviours was total school avoidance, refusal, or truancy and a number of reasons for such behaviours were revealed. Tom was clear about his motives for not attending school:

> "I thought I better not go into school, I might get bullied again."

Mike also explained why he did not want to go to school:

> "I didn't go to school 'cause I was scared to go into school."

Michael also described fear as a motive for not attending:

> "I didn't go to school four times once, 'cause I was too scared to go to school."

Another pupil explained:

> "I didn't go into mainstream school because of bullying."

These pupils were clearly more concerned with the anxiety and fear resulting from being in school than the problems or punishment that could result from non-attendance. Other pupils who described truanting appeared to be motivated by the potential rewards of conforming to the actions of a 'deviant' peer group. Such actions, often termed 'bunking', involved missing school and indulging in other activities with peers, many of which were antisocial and delinquent. Bobby explained:

No Win Situations

Certain behaviours may result from pupils feeling trapped in 'no win' situations.

Flight may be the only way to avoid escalation of a problem or further aggression.

Fear

Pupils may choose not to attend school because they are simply too frightened.

"Good the first couple of months then got to know a couple of people, you know, some of the bad ones, started skipping."

George explained:

"Me and my friends used to bunk off school. We used to go down [town] and spend our dinner money down the arcade and stuff. Walk around McDonalds."

Gerry offered insight into the fact that truanting may be a behaviour fuelled by peer pressure:

"I didn't know much about bunking off. One of my mates done it and I done it with him ... I bunked off about three weeks in a row."

Dave had a similar story:

"He said do you wanna go to school. I said, no not really. We done it once, then the second time about forty of us done it, and that's when we got caught."

The Peer Group

Joining a truanting peer group may provide greater rewards than attending school.

Both Gerry and Dave were boys finding the academic demands of their schooling difficult and the factors that they perceived as causing problems for them were related to the academic expectations of the school. It would seem reasonable to propose that both boys lacked self-esteem and reward from being in school. They appeared to seek rewards, a sense of belonging or even a certain degree of self-control by rejecting the school and its goals, replacing them with those offered by membership of a deviant peer group. It is not difficult to understand a pupil who misses school in favour of a day with friends, when one considers the relative personal gains and losses from each situation. Consider Dave's description of his typical behaviour in school:

"I didn't get on with lessons. I messed around."

His reason for messing around was:

"If I was stuck I couldn't do it."

Finally, he described the consequences for his actions:

"Sent me to the Headmaster's office and I had to stand out there all day."

However, learning difficulties and lack of academic stimulation or compensation for attending school do not account for all truanting. A further motive for truanting may simply have been a desire to avoid schoolwork. Ronnie and Julie described such avoidance, although they appeared to have had very different sub-motives. Ronnie appeared to find the curriculum and the goals of the school meaningless and irrelevant and he was confident that he could leave school and get a job regardless of school success:

"I'll get out. I'll start working. I'll earn £150 - £200. I'll have loads a nice clothes. That's all I think about."

Julie was a good example of a pupil not attending school because she felt unable to deal with the academic expectations and the subsequent humiliation or punishment that she feared would result. In contrast to Ronnie who appeared to see no value in school, Julie did want to learn but could not meet the demands placed on her, as her comments in chapter 3 demonstrate.

All of the pupils' statements in this section throw valuable light on the many varied yet rational responses given by pupils with EBD when asked to give motives for truancy. Much research has been carried out on truancy and absenteeism. In the mid-1980's Reid (1985) was particularly interested in this issue and researched pupils' perceptions, which was a move away from more traditional beliefs that truancy was simply a result of social background and class. His research revealed the importance of schooling factors in particular and encouraged educators to seek answers within their institutions. Other research has attempted to provide correlation between truancy figures and factors both inside and outside school. Pasternicki et al (1993) made a more recent study of in school factors linked to pupils' decisions not to attend. One interesting result was that truancy was more often a solitary activity than a result of group pressure, although those pupils who had not truanted did report having to resist group or peer pressure to do so. (p6). The pupils in this present study who described 'bunking', truanting or missing school were both solitary and in groups. This decision appears to depend largely on the source of the pupils' disaffection with school. The degree of isolation from peers that the pupil is experiencing is critical, combined with other factors linked to the pupils' value system and ability to meet the academic expectations of the school. Each case of truancy reflects the individual's own attempts to deal with a complex mixture of fears, needs and values.

Truancy or phobia?

When taking into account the pupils' perspectives of their motives for not attending school it becomes apparent that such behaviour is complex and more than a simple decision to avoid school. One problem for professionals is to determine the extent to which a pupil is simply choosing to not attend, perhaps in order to achieve some benefit from alternative actions, or whether that pupil actually considers him or herself unable to attend. This also leads to issues of whether to punish or empathise and whether to use the word truant or phobia. These two words used to label pupils carry different connotations in terms of the pupils' difficulties and level of responsibility for their behaviour. Truancy and particularly 'bunking' implies that the pupil has control and is electing to miss school possibly without 'good' reason. It is perceived as a 'deviant' action, where as phobia is a term insinuating an illness and possibly allowing a more sympathetic attitude. Montgomery (1989) describes truancy as; 'Wilful non-attendance at school often associated with social factors and alienation from school.' (p50) Phobia is described as follows; 'School phobia as the name signifies has as its base an emotional problem or state of emotional illness in which the pupil cannot attend school for fear of distressing, and even catastrophic emotional reactions which he/she cannot control.' (p50).

Avoiding School Work

Non attendance may be motivated by an irrelevant curriculum or fear of academic failure.

Pupils' Needs And Values

Avoiding school may be a way for pupils with EBD to meet complex needs and reflects their values.

Labelling

How we label a behaviour can affect our response to it.

Our beliefs regarding such issues are possibly linked to the theoretical stance we take in terms of behaviour. Clarizio (1992) suggests that the extent to which we believe emotional disturbance to have played a part in a child's behaviour affects how we label them. As previously described he proposes that a different attitude and education may be needed for socially maladjusted pupils as opposed to the seriously emotionally disturbed, a belief echoed by Vivian (1994). Chapter 3 described the way a label suggesting an emotional illness, psychological or physiological problem can be a useful escape route for professionals, parents and pupils alike.

Pupils' comments regarding their avoidance of, or flight from school through illness or psychosomatic symptoms, provides interesting insight into the extent to which such behaviour does differ from truancy. Five of the pupils described illness as a means to avoid school. Gerry and Sarah both admitted to creating or using their illness:

"I used to get up in the morning and say I don't feel well."

"I made myself ill."

Roy was not so sure of the origins of his illness each morning. He stated:

"I got mysteriously ill."

He continued:

"I'd wake up in the morning. I'd think about school and I'd feel ill. I was sick, my stomach felt like it was a lead weight."

Roy described his mother trying to get him to school:

"In the morning I'd try to go back to sleep. My Mum used to drag me out of bed, carry me down the stairs."

He described feelings of confusion and panic:

"I can't really remember my feelings, they were just a jumble, a mess. When I got in a panic at the bus stop and phoned my Mum, my mind was in a mess."

Illness

Pupils may use illness as a way to avoid school.

A medical diagnosis of a problem behaviour may shift the control of and responsibility for that behaviour away from the child.

Wayne tried to explain how his own feelings contrasted to those of others:

"You feel physically ill, but you're not in real life. It was real to me."

For Sarah the whole school created a problem for her and she defined the problem as a phobia:

"It's the fact that it's a school that had that effect on me."

Although she had described some minor peer problems and analysed her fear to include the size and nature of the buildings, she remained unable to rationalise her behaviour. Referral for psychiatric treatment appeared to justify her feelings and emotions.

The comments in this section certainly suggest that professionals should carefully consider the motives behind truancy or school refusal and should be particularly aware of how different labels can influence the attitudes and expectations of a pupil. Labelling can significantly alter a child's perceptions of his or her behaviour and the degree of control or responsibility for change that he or she should have over that behaviour.

Self harm

A serious behaviour that is somewhat difficult to categorise involves actual or threatening self harm. Four of the pupils described this as a behavioural response to their feelings including Susan:

> "I cut myself, when I got annoyed, when people annoyed me ... it gets all the anger out of me ... I don't do it to anyone else, I do it to me when I get angry."

Karen described her overdose, yet did not disclose completely why she did it:

> "I took an overdose ... that was something personal I never tell anyone why I done that."

Two other pupils, Sarah and Wayne, described threatening suicide but did not describe in any depth why they had done so:

> "I told my Mum I had suicidal feelings."

> "I said I'd commit suicide. I wouldn't but I said I would."

Connor (1994) comments on the work of Malcolm & Haddock (1992), who stress the importance of recognising withdrawal and self-injurious behaviours. (p9). They suggest that it may be girls who use such 'under-reacting' behaviours, as opposed to boys who 'overreact' when distressed, and that girls tend to be ignored because their behaviours have less impact than acting out behaviours. If extreme actions such as self harm are in any way related to school problems, and the pupils are resorting to such actions for lack of alternative outlets for their feelings and emotions, then clearly we must work towards providing safe ways for these pupils to communicate their needs.

Key points emerging from this section

- Each pupil's case story is unique yet their descriptions of behaviours are often similar.

- Pupils' descriptions of behaviours suggest that they feel frustrated by a lack of acceptable behavioural options when dealing with difficulties or emotions.

Self Harm

Pupils may harm themselves as a means to communicate problems.

- In many cases pupils' behaviours reflect a need to escape situations within the school setting.

- Pupils may perceive a lack of positive reward for remaining in school.

- Some pupils do not have a sense of belonging in school and instead may even experience fear and anxiety.

- Pupils with EBD respond to feelings of fear and not belonging with various behaviours that could be categorised as flight or withdrawal.

- Flight may be considered an understandable response to a stressful situation where basic needs are not being met.

Thoughts for your reflection

- When dealing with certain behaviours in your classroom are you aware that they may be attempts to escape fear, anger or embarrassment?

- Can you make any changes in your classroom or school to help avoid no-win situations for children from which they may want to escape or flee?

- Is it possible to create acceptable and legitimate opportunities for children to withdraw from certain situations in the classroom or school?

- Can you teach alternative behavioural skills allowing them to withdraw appropriately when necessary?

- Can you create a sense of belonging for every child in your school or classroom and ensure that there is something positive offered each day as a result of attending?

- Are the labels that you use for childrens' behaviour in anyway judgemental or presumptuous?

- Do you accept and believe that behaviour is a form or communication?

- How do you respond to this statement by Simon?:

    "There's always a reason behind everything and I'm not sure if the school really looks at all those reasons why it's happening. They only hear one side of the story and that's it."

4.2(ii) Fight

Fight

Behaviours of an aggressive, anti-social or disruptive nature can be considered as ways to fight the system.

In this section the word fight is used to denote a behaviour that may be aggressive, anti-social, disruptive or unacceptable. It is used to represent behaviours with which the pupils appear to reject or fight the expectations of the school system. The pupils' perceptions of such behaviours are presented and wherever possible their own interpretation of the motives or rationale behind these behaviours are given. As in the previous section the pupils' ability to interpret and rationalise their own behaviour varied a great deal. Some were only able to make simple descriptions of events and their own actions, whilst others had developed insights into situations and events, and showed awareness of why something had happened and the motives behind both their own and the actions of others.

The pupils' comments have been presented under two sub-headings based on their degree of aggression; those that were physically or verbally aggressive and those that were simply disruptive.

Aggressive behaviours

The pupils' comments regarding aggressive behaviours are closely linked to those concerned with social interaction in schools because they frequently focussed on problems associated with their peer group, including bullying and fighting. Pupils suggest that fighting may be an important way of achieving power, dominance, and status or to establish oneself at the top of the unwritten hierarchy within the peer group. Although closely linked to bullying it seems that fighting is not always synonymous with bullying. Of the thirty-six pupils interviewed in the study, twenty described fighting as a behaviour in which they had been involved, and which had contributed to their difficulties. It was however a behaviour described by the boys only, as none of the small number of girls interviewed described fighting as one of their behaviours. This result is in agreement with Mooney et al (1991) who found that more boys than girls fight in schools. The high occurrence of fighting as a behaviour for boys, and its acceptance as the norm in school settings, was pointed out by Simon:

"Kids fight, boys fight, it's natural."

Boulton (1993b) suggests that perhaps this fact is linked to the male need to be regarded as tough and hard. He suggests that fighting can be an '...overt demonstration of these qualities.' (p235). Boulton also refers to research which reveals that '...children looked positively on peers who use aggression to stand up for themselves...' (p240). Such results illustrate the very close similarities between bullying and fighting. If fighting enhances popularity then it may achieve the same as bullying, as Olweus (1994) states '...bullies do not reach the low level of popularity that characterizes the victims.' (p1180). However, although simple observation may suggest that fighting and bullying achieve similar goals, pupils' statements regarding these behaviours suggest differences in motive. Sam described his behaviour and motives:

"Fighting makes you popular with all the others. When I beat up R.B., I started to get respect from all the fifth years."

Sam does not describe repeated aggression towards one person, or an obvious desire to damage or hurt his victim. His action appears to be essentially concerned with his own popularity and status in the eyes of his peers. Dave was another boy who offered evidence that fighting may not be as malicious as bullying, just primarily concerned with status:

Fighting

Many boys consider fighting a normal part of life.

Fighting and Bullying

Although often similar in appearance these two behaviours may have different goals.

"When I see other people having a fight, I get stuck in, like showing off."

Karl also described the role of fighting as a means to establish himself within the pupil hierarchy:

Status through Fighting

Fighting may be more concerned with gaining status than hurting another person.

"I used to like fighting. I used to think I was really big. I wanted to be top dog of the school which like I was at the time. But I wanted to prove it. Every time a new kid came in, if he looked pretty hard I'd challenge him and smash him up. It was just a challenge. I did enjoy it, but it's not a good thing to do. It's like a boxer with his title."

Karl's behaviour does not seem to have the goal of hurting someone else at a deep emotional level but simply to prove supremacy of a physical nature. Simon gave an interesting example of how his own interpretation of his school behaviour differed from what others may have perceived:

"Sometimes I bully kids, although I don't look at it as bullying. What I call bullying is like when I was younger, my Mum used to have to pay the kids a pound a week not to beat me up. That is a form of bullying. If she didn't pay it I'd be riding along on my skateboard, I'd feel this baseball bat on the back of my head. They knocked me out cold. That's what I call bullying."

Different Perspectives

Using pupils' perspectives to better understand aggressive behaviours is essential.

The willingness and ability of the pupils with EBD in this study to reflect on their actions and give accounts of the motives and reasons behind them should encourage professionals to seek pupils' perspective prior to passing judgement on certain behaviours. This is particularly important if we consider the number of pupils who perceived that their aggression was driven by fear, insecurity or retaliation to provocation. The significance of such behaviour in the exclusion of pupils from mainstream schools as revealed by the pupils in this study should also fuel our desire to better understand it. In support of this statement, a three year study (Imich, 1994) shows that exclusions are going up, that four times as many boys than girls are being excluded, and nearly half of all exclusions are for verbal or physical offences against peers.

The pupils described aggressive behaviours as being primarily within the peer group. Aggression aimed at the system itself, including teachers, was much more unusual. Dave was a boy who admitted to being aggressive with peers and a teacher:

"I hit people. I pushed a teacher."

Jeremy, Michael and Brian, who was a 14 year old boy with learning difficulties, attending Southdown School as a result of disruptive and aggressive behaviours, also all described incidents involving aggression against teachers:

"I thumped the Head too."

"I kept on being naughty, throwing stuff at the teachers and all that and one of the teachers, I threw a pair of scissors at her and they hit her."

"I used to chuck chairs at teachers."

Aggression Against Teachers

A small number of pupils may physically assault teachers.

These boys all explained their actions as being a result of frustration in the classroom, and all were boys with some learning difficulties. Michael explained why he threw chairs:

"Work was too hard for me, and people winding me up and taking the Mick."

When he was asked why people 'took the Mick' he explained:

"I can't write properly, I couldn't spell properly."

Although this small number of boys described aggressive behaviour against teachers as their reaction to frustration in the classroom, it would appear that most pupils avoided this violent option, electing to adopt disruptive, acting out type behaviours in those situations.

Disruptive Behaviours

Disruptive behaviours appear to represent a fight with the rules and expectations of the school system and some examples of the behaviours termed disruptive have been described by pupils in chapter 3. A number of different behaviours can be considered to fall under the term disruptive including one frequently used term 'mucking about' or 'messing about'. Larry described his attitude to school:

Being Disruptive

A variety of behaviours can be disruptive including 'messing' around.

"I'd go for a laugh, muck around."

However Robin, a 16 year old boy at Southdown School who had been in a number of previous special needs facilities, including a psychiatric hospital, and who had displayed a variety of disturbing behaviours, made a statement which revealed how disruptive behaviours may also be very aggressive. He described his behaviour in class:

"Throwing things around. Swearing at teachers."

Pupils readily gave accounts of what they had done and some of the boys in the study offered the following descriptions of their behaviour:

"In science I turned on a gas tap and put a match in front of it."

"Throw rubbers at people and annoy them."

"Mucking about dancing on tables."

"I kept being naughty, throwing stuff at teachers and all that."

"I used to get told off quite a lot for playing jokes and not paying attention in class."

"I used to make noise, throw things about ..."

"I used to muck around in class a lot. I used to chuck rubbers, little bits of rubber, flicking at people, on a ruler."

There were also other types of behaviour which were not described as 'messing about' but involved rule breaking and lack of co-operation. Cooper et al (1994) use the word 'oppositional' to describe 'deliberate repeated infringement of classroom rules.' (p95). For the pupils in the present study these behaviours included not doing homework or not wearing the appropriate uniform. Sandra described her behaviour:

"I used to go into school in jeans. I used to wear my school uniform and my trainers which you're not supposed to do."

Smoking was another behaviour that had created friction between the pupils and their schools. Andy, Gerry, Larry and Ronnie all raised this as an issue for them within the mainstream setting:

"In them sort of schools you're not allowed to smoke. I used to go behind the science block. Teachers used to come round quite a lot and catch us."

"We were allowed out at lunchtime, teachers go for a cup of tea, we would go behind the huts."

Oppositional Behaviours

Some behaviours involve intentionally defying rules and expectation.

"In the fourth year people started smoking in school..."

"I got suspended because I started smoking puff in the bogs."

Dave actually commented that being allowed to smoke in the special school setting had reduced his school problems. When asked about the differences between mainstream and special provision, he replied:

"You can smoke."

Other behaviours that antagonised teachers and appeared to fall under the 'disruptive' umbrella were refusing to work, ignoring teachers and destroying work. Larry explained his behaviour:

"We were in it for a laugh. If we didn't like a lesson we wouldn't do it."

Other pupils described similar actions, yet for quite different reasons, such as not being able to do the work. Sandra also described destroying work:

"Well once I did my work and I screwed it up cause I didn't wannit. She told me off for not doing any work."

Antagonistic Behaviours

Certain unco-operative behaviours may irritate teachers although motives seem to vary.

Johnny was another low ability pupil who reacted in a similar way to Sandra:

"I just stopped doing my work, and when they told me I just couldn't do it. I just used to sit there and she'd tell me to get my maths book out, I'd just sit there. She'd grab me."

Of the different disruptive behaviours described, it is interesting to note that the boys in the study were the ones to describe 'mucking about', and not the girls, although clearly there were far fewer girls interviewed. This observation agrees with the proposal made by Measor & Woods (1984), that these behaviours are 'male preserves' (p116), and that strategies used by girls are less disruptive and more 'invisible'.

Defining 'disruptive' behaviours has been attempted and carried out by a number of other researchers and reports. The Elton Report (DES, 1989a) acknowledged the fact that disruption is not always in evidence as conspicuous, indisputable events, rather it may be 'a persistent low-level disruption' (p67) which actually wears teachers down and frustrates them. More recently, Miller (1994) also refers to those behaviours that may be perceived as trivial if taken in isolation, yet their persistent use results in problems. The pupils in this study were certainly able to describe their overtly 'disruptive' actions but were not apparently so aware of any more subtle behaviours that they may have displayed which teachers would perhaps classify as disruptive. However, it is clearly valuable to explore disruptive behaviours from the pupils' perspective as the motives behind their behaviour contain valuable information for school and classroom management strategies.

Having categorised and illustrated disruptive behaviours in terms of mucking about, rule breaking and lack of co-operation, it is also possible to categorise the motives that were given by pupils for their behaviour. Motives can be placed in various broad categories independent of the behaviours. Firstly, some of the pupils did reveal a basic and understandable need to socialise and have fun. As Bobby stated:

> "I just wanted a bit of fun at the time, just like nowadays really. If I wanted fun I'd just go out and cause a bit of mischief."

Ronnie also stressed the importance of fun in his life:

> "But I enjoyed myself, that's why I can't really regret my life at all so far because maybe I was a shit... and things did happen, but don't worry... I still enjoyed myself, it was quite a laugh."

The need for social interaction and to 'have fun' with other pupils, could be considered a legitimate human need. Tattum (1984) describes various motives for pupils' behaviour including, 'Everybody messes about - only having a laugh'. He suggests that the behaviour is not malicious, and is defined as disruptive only within a strongly rule bound institution. He also questions whether schools show enough consideration for the amount of time necessary for the social side of a young person's development. Barrett (1984) provides evidence to support these criticisms finding that pupils want laughs. One pupil described how they were expected to 'sit in silence for the whole day, ... and because you can't talk, you do talk - and you don't learn.' (p38). Miller (1994) similarly found that the disruptive pupils she interviewed considered that taking opportunities for socialising were 'entirely reasonable and appropriate'. (p238).

Gender Differences

Boys and girls may choose different behaviours to communicate their needs and feelings.

Defining 'Disruptive'

Even apparently minor and covert behaviours can be extremely disruptive.

Motives for Disruption

Pupils give various motives for their disruptive behaviours.

Having a Laugh

Some pupils simply want to interact with peers and have fun.

Boredom

Boredom may be described as a common reason for disruptive behaviour.

The pupils also revealed boredom and frustration as motives for 'messing around', talking, joking and laughing. Andy stated:

> "I used to get bored with school."

Pupils commonly perceive boredom as a justified motive for certain behaviours in school. School may be described as 'boring' by even the most successful pupil, not only those displaying difficult behaviours. However, it is clear that boredom or frustration can result from difficulties with classroom work particularly for pupils with EBD. They may perceive themselves as having too little to do, being unable to do the work owing to inadequate teacher support, or as simply unwilling to work, claiming that the material is irrelevant. These curriculum-related issues were discussed previously. The pupils' choice of behaviour as a result of these feelings seemed to provide them with preferable emotions or results. Bobby related his actions to needing attention:

> "It's when the work is really boring ... you wanna get attention. You get distracted especially when you're sitting there doing nothing."

He also described his inability to remain focused on work when his peer group distracted him, apparently offering something more interesting than the work itself:

> "Sometimes I think 'gotta get my head down', then as soon as something arises, like Ian broke the leg of a chair, that's it, I just get up, my concentration's gone."

Other pupils such as Dave and Johnny had learning difficulties and blamed their disruptive behaviour on a lack of support from teachers. Dave was quite specific about his motives for messing about:

Learning Difficulties

Pupils needing a lot of teacher support may become disruptive if they do not receive it.

> "If I was stuck, I couldn't do it."

Johnny explained:

> "I just wanted help and they just ignored me the teachers. I just started messing about."

Not being able to 'do' the work seems to lead to boredom or a void which needs to be filled. The pupils' perception of struggling with class work was sometimes inseparable from a belief that teachers do not offer enough support, ignore them, or that the work is inappropriate for their ability. Ken directly associated his behaviour with lack of time and attention from staff:

> "If they did help me, I still didn't understand then I'd mess about then. They just went and I'd mess about."

A comment about his special school supported the fact that his behaviour was closely related to the amount of support he received from teachers:

" ... smaller classes ... They don't ignore you so much as in other schools, so you don't have so much opportunity to mess about as much."

Montgomery (1989) describes the desire to relieve or replace unpleasant feelings of boredom or frustration as seeking 'cognitive exhilaration.' (p38). She quotes Reid (1986), in saying that; 'Excitement is probably the greatest spur to misbehaviour in classrooms for all our pupils. The more boring the lessons and the less involving they are, the more likely the pupils will feel alienated and need to seek other forms of excitement through disruption.' (p38). Seeking such excitement may be perceived as relatively uncontrollable in certain pupils, as Ken explained:

"But if one person plays up, then I think about joining in. I don't know why it is. Some magnet just drags me into trouble, I just can't help myself but to join in."

However, the curriculum and its inability to stimulate and reward, is unlikely to account alone for all disruptive behaviours. The pupils' need for excitement and stimulation is also closely linked to status and respect within the peer group which was previously described in depth as a motive for fighting and aggressive behaviour. This acceptance within certain peer sub-cultures was perceived by some pupils as being achievable through making others laugh and making jokes or by breaking the rules. John gave 'showing off' as a reason for his disruptive behaviour and Karl used the expression to explain his need to join in fights. Both suggest a need for recognition from others although George revealed an even more honest self-analysis of the reasons behind his behaviour:

" ... if I was not happy ... I was trying to hide it by acting and everything like that. They were acting the class fools and everyone liked them, so I thought if I acted the class fool everyone will like me."

George, who had been bullied, appeared to have been attempting to escape negative feelings and to survive by becoming popular with peers through joking. Measor & Woods (1984) believe that joking is '...one of the chief survival mechanisms' (p111). They suggest that there are 'bids for status and control, in the use of joking...' (p109). This is similar to the observations of Miller (1994) who describes pupils she interviewed as undertaking '...the role of "class clown" in order to appear "normal"...' (p241). The need to be perceived as 'normal' is clearly closely linked to the need to identify with the majority and not stand out in isolation as an individual or deviant, an experience that holds the potential to trigger victimisation. Larry described his experiences when starting at a new school following bullying problems at a previous school. He illustrates how powerful the behaviour of well established peer groups can be on individuals who are anxious to conform:

"At that school when I first went there everyone was pissing about so I thought it's OK to piss about. It seemed like the normal thing to do."

Johnny described disruptive behaviour in the classroom in terms of peer pressure and conforming to the norm:

Seeking Excitement

Misbehaviour may be attributed to seeking some form of excitement.

"Because you used to get a ruler, put a piece of rubber on it and fire it over. I used to do that all the time. They got me to do it. They didn't make me do it, but I felt I was being left out. So I done it."

Other rule breaking behaviours, such as stealing, smoking or drinking also appear to be attempts to gain acceptance from peers, and to maintain self-esteem under peer pressure. Tom described drinking alcohol in school to be a part of a group who encouraged him to do so:

Showing Off

Joking or breaking rules may be attempts to impress peers.

"I thought I'd try it, everyone thinks I'm a weed and so I thought I'd try it."

Smoking has been described earlier as a rule breaking activity for many pupils with EBD. Michell & Fidler (1993), studied the social significance of smoking to boys in an EBD residential school, and found not only a high percentage of smokers (93%) but also that smoking helped define these boys as '...tough, aggressive anti-establishment.' (p58).

The need to retain or gain self-esteem did not appear to involve only the peer groups and their values or opinions. There also appeared to be a need for recognition and respect from teachers and the school system itself, and in a number of cases this was perceived as missing in mainstream schools. Larry described how his behaviour reflected his frustration at not being involved in choices or consulted on decisions in school. He described a dislike of the formal procedures of the school, such as sitting in alphabetical order, and being told what to do:

"He thought he could say 'you do this' and we'd do it like robots ... He doesn't realise that you are people."

He continued:

"They try to manipulate ya, ... try to intimidate ya."

Feeling Important

Pupils can seek to retain or regain power through their behaviours.

Larry appeared to describe a feeling of losing control in school, reflecting a lack of status and respect for pupils. The removal of the pupils' autonomy and power may be reflected in their behavioural attempts to regain it. Larry's subsequent descriptions of his behaviour illustrate how these attempts can simply create further loss of respect in the eyes of teachers and tighter discipline. He described his relationship with staff:

"It was like a constant fight."

He continued:

"It's just when they say you have to work. It feels like you're being bossed about, then you start doing the opposite to what they say. It becomes a habit really."

In Larry's case doing the opposite to what he was told seemed to be a mis-guided attempt to regain some control over his own actions. Unfortunately such disruptive behaviour usually achieves quite the opposite resulting in even tighter controls and discipline. Similarly pupils' attempts to gain attention or respect from school staff can often be misinterpreted. Miller (1994) describes the way disruptive behaviours such as calling out answers are explained by bright disruptive pupils as being simply ways of letting the teacher know that they knew the answers. They did not seem to be aware of the disruptive nature of their actions although the teachers themselves described it as 'showing off' or 'just being clever.' (p246). Such misinterpretation of behaviour and motive is not something for which teachers alone are guilty. Some of the pupils themselves gave examples of their own subjective interpretation of teachers' actions. For example some low ability pupils would respond aggressively to being corrected or helped by a teacher. Although clearly not the intention of the teacher, some support may result in an undermining of the pupils' self-esteem and status and this dictates their response. Brian described his feelings:

> "Teachers got on my nerves. If I did something wrong and they told me to do it right or something, so I just got annoyed with them and started taking it out on them."

Misundertanding Behaviour

Both teachers and pupils may misinterpret behaviours and their intentions.

Some pupils expressed dissatisfaction with their relationships with the adults in the school and a lack of opportunity to be seen as equals, and this frustration appeared to motivate certain behaviours. The willingness of teachers to relax traditional roles and build adult type relationships with pupils can possibly make some difference to their pupils' attitudes and behaviour. However, it remains debatable to what extent lower ability pupils benefit from this more informal teacher role or are frustrated by this issue, as it is the brighter pupils both in this and other studies who raised it as being important to them.

Relationships with Teachers

Some pupils' behaviour reflects an attempt at building an adult type relationship with teachers.

Another motive for disruptive behaviour described by one pupil, was an attempt to escape from reality, and lose negative or difficult feelings. Roy described 'mucking around' as a way to escape and to forget his problems:

> "I muck about to forget things."

Escaping Reality

Pupils may behave in ways that help them to forget the reality of the situation they are in.

Measor & Woods (1984) may help understand exactly how such behaviour helps a pupil when they suggest that mucking about is the pupil's attempt 'to disrupt the official reality and redefine situations.' (p113). This idea may help explain a great deal of behaviour described as disruptive, offering an answer to 'how' the behaviour itself actually takes care of the problem. There may however be much simpler and more obvious motives that should not be overlooked in a search for an understanding of disruptive behaviour. For example Danny described previously how he achieved his goal of being thrown out of school by not doing detentions. Similarly Dave started to behave badly in the last year of Middle School because of a fear of moving into a new school:

> "I didn't want to go up. When I first heard about it from my mates a little older than me, I didn't wanna go there."

Achieving a Goal

Misbehaviour may be perceived as the only way to achieve a specific goal.

These clear and direct motives demonstrate how behaviour can be used to achieve very specific goals. For Dave, disruptive behaviour was perceived as

A New Start

Some pupils misbehave with a specific goal of being expelled and given a new start in a new school.

a way to prevent a move to another school. For Danny, it appeared to be a way to be expelled from a school situation that he perceived as offering little chance of success or reward, and in fact was often humiliating and frustrating. Danny's attempt to manipulate the system and be officially expelled from school may be typical of a small number of pupils who wish to 'start again' and be moved to a different school. Whether suffering pressure from peers of a social nature, such as bullying, or whether experiencing conflict with their school or teachers, the need to escape and regain a new identity in another place was perceived by some pupils as the only solution to their problems. This desire to make a new start appeared to result from the fact that some of the pupils perceived themselves as having acquired an unwanted label within the institution. Expectations of them and their behaviour had become fixed in certain ways and were driving or controlling their behaviour and interfering with change. These ideas are well documented as labelling theories and recent research has continued to reveal them as important when considering the behaviour of pupils within EBD in schools. The importance of these theories, from the perspective of the pupils interviewed in this present study, is discussed in the following section.

Key points emerging from this section

- Many pupils with EBD adopt behaviours that may be loosely termed 'fight' within the school setting.

- Aggressive or disruptive behaviours that pupils display in schools may have a number of different motives depending on the individual's needs or goals.

- The goal of the pupil is often to simply survive.

- Behavioural skills and choices available to pupils may be limited.

- Understanding the motives behind aggressive or disruptive behaviour may be the key to assisting teachers in responding more effectively.

Thoughts for your reflection

- Do you believe that pupils are in control of their own behaviours?

- To what extent do you think that pupils are responding to environmental pressures when they choose to behave in certain ways?

- Do you carefully consider the possible motives behind a pupil's behaviour and how they may be trying to meet specific needs through their behaviour?

- Are there any changes to your own classroom or school that could help a challenging pupil get his or her needs met more appropriately?

- Are any of your own behaviours contributing to a child's behaviour problems?

- Do you try to help difficult pupils by teaching behaviours that would enable them to get their needs met in an appropriate manner?

4.2 **How behaviours evolve and are labelled**

Labelling children and their behaviours

A number of the pupils who were interviewed made interesting statements regarding how being given a label for their behaviour and carrying a reputation had affected their subsequent actions. A whole theory of behaviour has in fact developed which explains deviance in terms of labelling. As a theory, labelling was originally developed in the 1960's by Kitsuse (1962) and Becker (1963) and has been adapted and developed since, stressing the importance of contextual consideration for behaviour and the fact that its interpretation is largely subjective. Fontana (1985) relates this theory to the classroom by stating that '...problem behaviour is only problem behaviour because it appears so to the teacher.' (p359). He continues by saying; 'And since teachers are all individuals, what may appear to be a problem to one teacher may not appear so to another.' (p359). Thus, a deviant act is only deviant in a specific context, where the rules and expectations of that context, possibly even of a whole society, define it as such. As Fontana (1985) suggests; '...problem behaviour... is in a sense in the eye of the beholder.' (p360).

Andy gave an interesting and valuable perspective on how he had begun to feel within his mainstream school prior to attending the Oakwood Centre:

> "I knew I'd bodge it all up ... I thought that the slightest thing I did wrong I'd have to go up to the head of year's office and be chucked out straight way."

He perceived his only escape to be a new chance:

> "I'd wanted to leave and go to a different school."

Harris (1994) discovered that pupils, particularly in bottom sets, had '...internalised negative messages from peers and teachers.' (p65), and Dave gave a good example of this:

> "They used to tell me I was thick so I thought I was thick."

He proudly explained how his move to a special school had since proved this 'label' to be wrong:

> "My old school told me I was behind, I was stupid and things like that. I came here and I'm on G4 [Maths]. My cousin who's older, she's on G4."

Alan felt that his reputation within the school had resulted in the teachers turning to him whenever bad behaviour or a problem occurred:

> "As soon as something went wrong he'd come to me first."

Scherer et al (1990) also believe this to be a problem for certain children stating, '...pupils considered to be deviant will be regarded with suspicion and their behaviour closely monitored.' (p110). Larry added to this argument:

Labelling Behaviours

Defining or labelling a behaviour as deviant depends on its context and who is judging that behaviour.

Carrying a Reputation

Pupils may develop reputations for certain behaviours that they find hard to lose.

133

"We wouldn't be doing anything and they'd pick on us anyway ... we'd think we'll do our work today and we'd say 'where's our work?', and they'd say 'you won't do any anyway'."

It would seem that the reputation that Larry and his friends had developed resulted in teachers' expectations of them being very low. It is possible that the teachers had become cynical which was interfering with attempts by pupils to lose or change their disruptive behaviour.

One possible behavioural response to being labelled as deviant is for the pupil to decide to live up to that reputation. Larry explained:

"They'd say things like, 'you're not worth the time' ... that's when I started to get suspended etc, or I'd bunk off just to avoid the hassle."

He supports Scherer et al (1990) who suggest that 'labelling may produce a self fulfilling prophecy.' (p11). They continue by saying; 'A child who is aware that the 'deviant' label has been applied may behave especially well in order to have the label removed, or may accept the label and behave accordingly.' (p11).

Karen considered that discipline procedures in schools allow certain disruptive pupils to intentionally create deviant reputations for themselves, providing status for themselves amongst their peers:

Expectations for Behaviour

Labels may serve to impact the expectations for behaviour held by the child and teachers.

"It gives people a reputation, and they're gonna do it even more, or maybe they think, well if that's the way they think I'm gonna act, I will."

As previously explained, some pupils perceived a new start, perhaps in a new school to be the only way forward. This change would allow them to leave their unwanted reputation with peers or teachers behind them. In Cooper's (1989) work with pupils with EBD in residential schooling he describes the way in which the identity of these children can become fixed in the eyes of others. He suggests that one of the roles of the EBD residential school is to offer an opportunity for 're-signification' or the changing of a negative identity into a new positive one. Some pupils both in Cooper's study and at the Oakwood Centre and Southdown perceived the special school setting as offering a welcome opportunity for re-signification. They believed that their reputations as disruptive, aggressive, bully, victim etc., could be left behind when they moved to a new school and their behaviour in that new environment would not be influenced by the expectations of peers or teachers based on past experiences. Bobby described people's responses to him in the mainstream setting:

"At my old school, once people get to know you, the way you really are, they don't wanna know you really."

Alan felt that one of the differences in the special setting compared to mainstream was in the way teachers treated the pupils:

"Everyone being treated equal. The teacher not having favourites."

Karen also tried to convey her positive feelings about the special school and what made it different. Interestingly she perceived that it was the fact that peers and teachers were familiar with her problems and difficulties in that setting that made it successful and special for her, which may be in contrast to other pupils who wanted to lose reputations:

> "Everyone knows you, everyone knows that this is your problem ... they know that you've got a problem, they're not gonna hassle you by giving you more. I think it's just a bit more thoughtful."

Some pupils did not find that a new school offered them an opportunity to make changes and lose an unwanted reputation. Alan explained:

> "I went there with a reputation."

He then continued by describing his experiences of the new school:

> "Everybody knew me, like all the prefects ... I'll be top of the list. When I went there I was top of the list to get expelled. ... I didn't like it but I was stuck with it."

George described his experiences after moving to a new school:

> "Mr. Smith, the Deputy Head, if there were any fights or whatever at school, he always used to blame me and my friends ... It's like the area we come from is really rough. My mate, my friends, none of us like had a good report from before."

Interestingly he linked his social life out of school to the way he was treated in school. Coming from a rough area of council housing, he stated:

> "I've got a name around the streets."

These comments support the findings of Gersch & Nolan (1994) who interviewed a small number of excluded pupils. 'They sometimes felt that the teacher took an immediate dislike to them and then interpreted everything they did negatively. This happened particularly when the pupil was going into his/her second or third school and thus arrived with an "excluded" label.' (p39). These problems refer to pupils transferring between mainstream schools, yet transfer to a special school may also create problems. The decision to place a pupil in a special setting clearly establishes and makes official the EBD label. Just as the formal structure of the mainstream school can play its part in labelling when streaming or grouping takes place, so a special school placement could be considered to be the extreme end of a spectrum of labelling measures providing or confirming negative identities for certain pupils. The impact of such a label on a pupil may be extremely powerful as it is usually issued by 'experts' who determine the needs of the child. A number of pupils commented on the stigma attached to being placed in a special school. Julie stated:

> "You go to a special school, you must be thick."

A New Start

Moving to a new school may be seen as a way to lose an unwanted or damaging reputation.

Being Targeted

Some pupils feel targeted in a new school owing to previous behaviours.

Special School Placement

A special school placement may be considered as a very powerful form of labelling.

135

Gerry had been moved into a special school when he was at Junior School. At that stage he had severe learning difficulties but had also developed behaviour problems. His comments during the interview suggested that he had been confused and upset by the decision to move him into special education. Until that time he had been in school with his twin brother and he described how it felt to lose the support that his brother had given him, both socially and academically. He also described the stigma and embarrassment he felt at attending a special school that was close to his previous mainstream school:

> "I used to hate that school so much ... We used to get off the bus right outside R. School, and everyone used to know me there and it was so embarrassing."

For Gerry the placement created a feeling of isolation that did not appear to alleviate any previously established feelings of inadequacy, or of being different. He stated:

> "I do feel left out ... They seem to get all the fun, because it's a bigger school, there's more of them."

Disadvantages of Special Education

Attending a special school can be stigmatising for certain pupils and may impact social interaction with peers and family.

Are Special Schools The Answer?

The value of placing a child in a special school is open to debate.

The social disadvantages associated with attending a special school were also recognised by Sarah and Roy. Sarah travelled daily to the Oakwood Centre from her home and felt distanced from her local community:

> "There's no friends nearby to come around."

Roy felt that the small size of the Oakwood Centre limited his social opportunities with friends:

> "I miss out on friends."

Susan also described how she perceived her placement at the Oakwood Centre to have affected the attitudes and behaviour of others towards her:

> "Cause it's a special school and it's different. They think there's something wrong with you, then they start feeling wary and then the teasing starts."

As Cooper (1989) suggests, it seems that a special school placement can alleviate many of the difficulties that pupils with EBD experience in a mainstream setting. Residential schools can offer the opportunity for 'respite' and 're-signification'. In contrast, the special school placement may also have the potential to contribute significantly to the labelling process, reinforcing a pupil's already negative perception of him or herself. Special school provision may be more concerned with the goals of educators, in removing disruptive elements and gaining 'homogeneity' of pupil groups, rather than actually meeting the needs of children. (Conner, 1994 p8).

Evolution of problem behaviour

Labelling theory can also be used to explain the way in which behaviours of children with EBD may evolve and develop. In fact Scherer et al (1990) propose that labelling theories can account for the development of certain behaviour patterns more readily than they can account for their origins. Hargreaves, Hester & Mellor (1975) describe one illustration of the concept of labelling theory, that is Lemert's (1967) theory of 'secondary deviance'. This theory considers that the social reaction to a deviant act creates a new problem for the person committing the act that he or she attempts to resolve by further, or secondary, deviant acts. Of importance is the fact that the secondary act does not have the same motives as the first act, it is concerned with attempting to find a solution to the problem created by the social reaction to the first. This social reaction may be punishment, stigma, isolation, creating feelings of embarrassment, anger or fear. Such feelings demand a behavioural response from most people to restore some balance or self-respect and in the case of pupils with EBD such responses are often limited and inappropriate. Charlton & David (1993) suggest that this creates '...a circular chain of increasingly negative interaction' (p115) which neither teacher or pupils can readily escape. Cooper (1989) also describes the circular nature of these interactional patterns as 'a circle of negativity.' (p47). He suggests that the chains of causation for behaviour are complex and 'create difficulties for those who attempt to understand and cope with the outcomes of the chain.' (p47). As Charlton & David (1993) say, it is difficult to know where to try to punctuate the circle. The circular nature of some behaviours was recognised and described by Larry who stated:

"It's a vicious circle really."

Larry appeared to feel trapped within a negative spiral of evolving behaviour, from which he had neither the skills, knowledge, or opportunity to escape. He described how as a result of being given detentions for his behaviour in school he then chose to miss school to avoid them, and thus was given further detentions. Eventually the number of detentions he had to do increased so much that he stopped going to school completely. Clearly the school's response to the behaviour that a pupil adopts in dealing with his or her initial problems may trigger secondary deviance. This secondary behaviour then becomes the main concern and focus for schools struggling with many cases of pupils who are challenging or disruptive. The initial trigger or problem may have been long lost amidst the escalating secondary behaviours.

Triggers for problems

We have seen in previous chapters how difficult it can be for the pupils themselves, or outside observers, to identify just one factor that had precipitated or triggered the pupils' problem behaviours. Charlton & David (1993) agree '...it is difficult - if not impossible - to isolate a *single* factor which was the sole cause of *all* the problem behaviours. While it may be possible to point to one particular factor which triggered the problem initially, others were certainly contributory.' (p22). Wayne was certainly unable to describe a reason for severe bullying:

"I don't know why they started bullying me, they just did."

Michael did however have an explanation for his behaviours:

Secondary Deviance

Teacher responses to misbehaviour may trigger or reinforce further deviancy.

Cycles of Negativity

Pupils can become caught in patterns of misbehaviour.

137

"I threw chairs, the work was too hard for me, and people winding me up and taking the Mickey ... I can't write properly, I couldn't spell properly."

George also had a clear perception of the triggers for his problems, and gave a valuable illustration of how one factor may initiate a chain reaction of 'deviant' behaviours, each attempting to alleviate problems created by the school or social response to the previous action. The trigger was his surname as previously described, which had a negative social connotation, leaving him vulnerable to ridicule:

"Half the kids at school didn't like me much ..."

When he was younger he had not been aware of any problems associated with his name:

"I don't think anyone really bothered at Middle School. They just thought a name's a name sort of thing."

"When younger, too young to know what the word meant..."

Wayne also tried to explain how his experiences of bullying had escalated as he got older:

"It was like Middle School when it started to hit, cause people like didn't understand, you know when you're young you don't really do bullying, people don't know what it is. But when you start to hit Middle School, you start getting attitudes, that's when it starts."

Triggers for Problems

It can be difficult to identify just one factor or triggering event although some pupils do have a clear perception of where or how their problems began.

He explained:

"I was getting older, and as I got older, I understood what they were saying. Before I didn't know what the hell they were talking about ... they didn't know what the hell they were talking about, but then they got things that they knew would hurt me, about my parents, definitely about my parents."

George's story continues with his transfer to a secondary school. Clearly someone had become aware of the problems he would encounter or had been encountering owing to his last name:

"Got my name changed just before I went there."

However, it appears that a reputation had already been established and there were other pupils from the Middle School also transferring to the new school:

"Cause I knew some other children ... and they told everyone in my class about what my name was and things like that, and it just started from there."

George was teased about his name and his subsequent behaviour reflected his attempts to deal with this problem. He described trying to become part of a popular peer group, and to join the bullies rather than be victimised and also numerous attempts to belong, be liked, and to protect himself from what Cooper (1989) calls 'the ultimate social failure of isolation.' (p53). However, in the eyes of his teachers, George was simply a disruptive and difficult pupil. His behaviour within school was generally unacceptable to the school, resulting in punishments and detention. In trying to avoid bullying and isolation he escalated conflict with the school itself and he recalled the bullying problems also increasing:

> "It just got worse and worse. Got to the stage where I didn't wanna go to school."

> "I used to ignore them half the time, then it used to get under my skin and really annoy me. Then I never used to go to school. They'd take the Mickey out of what my name used to be."

George's comments help to illustrates how the behaviours of a pupil with EBD evolve and clearly show how one triggering factor can result in a chain of well motivated, rational behaviours, which themselves then become the problem. It is possible that the behaviour of other pupils could also be analysed in this way revealing a similar pattern of evolution.

Key points emerging from this section

- Labelling may be considered a broad concept impacting how behaviours and pupils are named and described, how pupils are statemented and decisions regarding educational placement.

- Labelling pupils can significantly affect teachers' attitudes, responses and expectations of certain pupils and may make them feel stigmatised.

- How professionals respond to challenging behaviours can determine whether negative cycles of behaviour evolve.

- Secondary behaviour problems may develop when responses to initial problems are inappropriate.

- Some pupils carry reputations from past events or behaviour and therefore feel targeted by peers or professionals.

- Pupils may be desperate to be given the opportunity to leave a negative or problematic reputation behind them.

Thoughts for your reflection

- Do you think that it is essential for teachers to be aware of a pupil's social and educational history in order to work successfully with that child?

- Are your attitudes to difficult pupils ever influenced by your knowledge of their previous placements or behaviours?

- When you respond to a challenging pupil in your classroom are you aware of the underlying needs of the child or the possible triggers for their behaviour?

- Are you aware that the way a pupil responds to you may be a response to how you respond to their initial behaviour?

- Do you believe that a change in how you perceive a certain behaviour or how you approach or respond to a pupil may be the only way to break a cycle of negative behaviour?

- Be aware that certain behaviours may have the intent of escalating a situation in order that the child be removed from your classroom or school.

4.3 How children look for support and understanding

Looking for Support

Pupils appear to recognise their need for support and often do look for it when they have problems.

Many of the pupils described attempts they had made to seek support and someone to talk to about their problems. They appeared to have made legitimate attempts to survive and to 'solve' their problems in an acceptable way. In particular, a small number of pupils described their attempts to seek support from teachers or other school staff in informal ways. Whether this informal support was chosen in preference to more formal counselling support structures on offer within the school is difficult to assess. The pupils rarely talked of using formal support in the mainstream school so it is quite possible that none existed, forcing them to seek more informal relationships. For example Susan found the school nurse a helpful support:

> "The school nurse, she would always see me and talk to me."

Johnny found his only ally in the form of the school secretary:

> "There was a school secretary. I used to be really good friends with her and when I used to get into trouble, sent out of class, get sent to the secretary's office, I used to help her undo the boxes and that."

Wayne managed to find a relationship with one of the teachers, with whom he felt comfortable talking:

Informal Support

Pupils may seek out supportive adults in the school who are not necessarily teachers.

> "I went to Mrs. E., who was one person I could always talk to."

Pupils seeking support expressed quite simple needs, including someone to talk to, or someone who had the time or took the time to listen. Chris was a slow learner and he described his frustrating mainstream experiences, which finally resulted in him becoming a school refuser:

> " ... if you get too much pressure on you, you think I can't do this. I've told the teacher loads of times. Why does he not listen to me?"

Julie described her frustration at trying to talk to teachers about her academic problems in class:

"People didn't listen to me. They didn't listen to what I was saying. When I was saying it was too hard they were just ignoring me. That's what it felt like anyway."

She stressed the importance to her of finding someone who would listen:

"All of the teachers, none of them really listened."

Julie was also frustrated by promises of support that never materialised:

"The headmaster was supposed to be sending me to another school for a few days a week to help, but that never went through."

"They said they'd give me less homework but it seemed to be the same."

She continued by explaining how her problem began to escalate, with her getting into trouble for not completing work and also feeling inadequate:

"... they didn't explain nothing to ya. Then you had to take it in the next couple of days. If it wasn't done then you used to get into trouble."

"I felt stupid cause I couldn't do the work."

Julie finally became a school refuser:

"I fell behind on all my work, so I stopped going to school."

In addition to a perceived lack of support for academic needs, some of the pupils in the present study were also unhappy with the level of support they had received when suffering peer problems, Susan stated:

"I couldn't go and tell the teachers, 'cause they don't do anything."

Sarah commented on the teachers' lack of willingness to develop informal relationships with pupils from which the pupils could gain support and understanding:

"Most teachers tend to alienate you, treat you as if you're there to learn and not as anything else. Teachers are not human, they may be out of school but not in school."

Finally Wayne criticised teachers who did not have the time to talk:

"Always something else to do.... you can never get hold of them."

Some of the pupils in the study perceived peer support as having helped maintain them in the mainstream setting when adult support had failed or was perceived as unavailable. In a previous section pupils' difficulties relating to classroom expectations and the curriculum were described, and their strategies

Someone to Talk to

Pupils' needs may be simple, such as finding someone with the time to listen to them.

Inadequate Implementation of Support

Pupils are sometimes frustrated when promises of individualised programs are not followed up.

Building Supportive Relationships

Teachers may be reluctant to or lack the time to build informal supportive relationships.

Peer Support

Pupils value the support of their peers when coping with classroom pressures.

for dealing with such problems were presented. For pupils unable to cope with the academic pressures of the school system their peers were often perceived as a valuable resource. Using peers for support had either solved the problem of inadequate contact time with the teacher, or may have disguised weaknesses and prevented humiliation or vulnerability. Julie and Sandra perceived peer support as essential for their survival in the classroom. They believed it to have helped them to avoid failure or having to reveal inadequacy. Sandra explained:

> "It depends who's actually in the classroom. There's a girl the same age as me, having the same difficulties as me, so we used to try and help each other. If we were having any difficulties we'd tell the teacher. But she never used to be in my class all the time, I used to have all the brainy ones... I didn't wanna say nothing."

Julie explained how her problems in school had not been evident in her early schooling when she always had friends to support her:

> "Cause I used to have help then. Always someone with me."

She described the support she received:

> "It's nice when your friends explain it to ya."

> "If I couldn't do it they used to help me, or I'd sit and copy the work."

Removing Support

In the secondary school the support of peers may be less acceptable creating problems for certain pupils who have relied on it in previous schools.

Behaviour problems may arise when the teaching techniques of secondary schools and their testing procedures remove critical peer support structures that have nurtured pupils such as Sandra and Julie through earlier schooling. Sandra explained how things changed for her a few months after going to secondary school:

> "Cause if you're stuck and you chat to your friends they can help you. But sometimes you can't do that, you're not allowed to chat to your friends, if they can help you. Or if you're working in two's, you're not allowed to talk. I don't like that."

For both girls, missing school was perceived as preferable to facing humiliation or punishment for not doing their class work and both stopped attending.

Key points emerging from this section

- Pupils with EBD do recognise their need for support and do seek out opportunities to discuss their problems.

- Informal support from adults may be equally as important or helpful to pupils as formalised counselling by designated professionals.

- Adequate support may not always be available in schools where teachers are busy and lack the time to listen and talk with troubled pupils.

- It is important that individualised needs are recognised and when programmes of support are planned that they are put into practice.

- Pupils may develop behaviour problems when peer support is removed.

Thoughts for your reflection

- Can you or do you make time for pupils to develop informal supportive relationships with you?

- Do you consider it your job to listen to pupils about problems they may be having both in or outside of school?

- Do you recognise the importance of peer support for certain pupils and do you think it is possible to build effective opportunities for such support in your classroom without it being detrimental to the pupils?

- Do you make every effort to follow through with individualised programmes or modifications designed for pupils having difficulties?

Some final thoughts from chapter 4

- Pupils with EBD are in many cases able and willing to describe and discuss their own behaviour.

- The knowledge gained from the pupils concerning their behaviour and also the actual process of talking with pupils holds significant potential for schools and professionals trying to meet their needs.

- The use of the words 'flight' or 'fight' to describe pupils' behaviours signifies the importance of survival for these pupils.

- It is not always possible to find consistent patterns or consistent links between behaviours and specific factors or situations as pupils do not necessarily respond to problems in the same way.

- There appear to be a limited number of behavioural options available to pupils facing difficulties, but they each have unique and complex individual needs .

- Pupils varied widely in their ability to analyse and make statements about their behaviour or rationalise it in terms of motive or gain.

- Language may be a frustrating factor for pupils trying to use words and expressions to describe their behaviours and feelings.

- For many pupils the motive for their behaviour was related to surviving stressful situations.

- The behaviour of pupils with EBD may be motivated by finding safety or by seeking some form of equilibrium in environments that threaten or intimidate them.

- Pupils with EBD may differ from successful mainstream pupils in their lack of coping skills or behavioural strategies.

- Pupils with EBD possibly experience somewhat more complex combinations of stresses in their lives making them more vulnerable to the demands of school.

- A complex combination of stressful factors within and outside of the school may combine with possible predisposing factors associated with a pupil's personality or temperament to create unmanageable emotional and behavioural demands.

- Behaviours of pupils with EBD can lead to responses from teachers that reinforce or fuel negative behaviours and attitudes, setting up cycles of disturbing behavior.

- Certain precipitating events or factors may trigger a cycle of disturbing behaviours.

- It is important that professionals consider pupils' behaviour in depth, and be willing to explore the motives behind it.

- Seeking clues as to the goal of a behaviour and what a pupil is gaining from the behaviour is an important responsibility for the professionals working with them.

- A willingness and desire to seek pupils' own perspectives on their behaviour, should encourage professionals to respond more sensitively to difficult behaviour, and to create more acceptable alternatives for these pupils which help them to achieve the same goal.

- We must seek to better understand the pupils' realities, without considering them impaired or invalid in some way.

Conclusion

I carried out this research project because there appeared to be little evidence of studies attempting to explore the perceptions of pupils with EBD of the many factors that may possibly have influenced their behaviour and lives. I set out to allow pupils who had struggled in the mainstream setting to give free responses to questions regarding the range of factors that may have influenced them and their behaviour. I hoped that my results could have implications both for preventing certain behaviours in schools and also for the nature of the support offered to pupils who struggle in that setting. This book is the culmination of my endeavours. Since I carried out this project there has been a growing interest in this field and it appears that seeking pupil perspectives is gaining more and more momentum. I simply hope that my contribution can make a small difference in our ability to support children who struggle in schools and help them to meet their true potential.

Appendix

Each of the trigger questions was designed to elicit pupil perspectives that would be pertinent to one of the areas of enquiry. The five areas of enquiry were proposed using information gained from an extensive review of the literature and previous research concerning various aspects of the behaviour of pupils with emotional and behavioural difficulties, including theoretical proposals. From this review emerged a number of recurrent themes pertaining to the behaviour of pupils with EBD, particularly relating to their experiences of schooling. These topical issues represent important areas that appear to influence the pupils' behaviour and are in many ways associated with the various systems that impact on that behaviour. Thus in order to allow some degree of focus on these relevant topical themes, they were utilised in the construction of the five areas of enquiry. It was anticipated that by allocating pupil statements to each of these areas of enquiry that the data could then be further analysed to provide a richer source of information relevant to significant issues reflected in and currently being raised in the literature.

Analysis of the pupil interview data was effectively carried out in three stages with an increasing degree of focus on the data at each stage. Firstly, a collating of statements for the areas of enquiry was carried out, with all pupil statements that were considered in any way relevant or insightful to a particular area of enquiry being selected. Secondly, statements were scrutinised more closely to ensure that they were appropriately assigned to an area, which was followed by a further analysis of these statements to identify different themes that were emerging. Finally, a further refinement and expansion of these emerging themes and preliminary ideas was undertaken, with a particular emphasis on placing them and the present research within the framework and context of previous and current literature and research concerned with the behaviour of pupils with EBD.

The questions used during the interviews as they related to each area of enquiry are as follows:

The history and nature of the pupils' schooling difficulties

- What are your earliest memories of school?

- Can you remember when you first had difficulties of any kind in school?

- Can you describe the problems that you experienced?

Aspects of school and schooling associated with the pupils' difficulties

- Can you talk about the sorts of things that happened in school that you found difficult or that were a problem for you?

The significance of social, family or life events in the pupils' difficulties

- Do you think that your problems in school have anything to do with your life or things that have happened out of school?

- What would you describe as the most important things that have happened to you in your life so far?

The psychological or physiological aspects of the pupils' difficulties and their attitudes to treatment or professional support

- How would you describe yourself to someone who didn't know you?

- Can you tell me about any help or support that you have had from people?

- How do you feel about having been placed in a special school?

The behaviour of the pupils in response to their difficulties

- When you were having difficulties or problems in school what did you do or how did you behave?

- Can you say anything about why you behaved in certain ways?

- Do you blame anyone or anything in particular for your behaviour and placement in a special school?

- Why do you think you are in a special school?

REFERENCES

ANGUS, L. (1993). "The sociology of school effectiveness." British Journal of Sociology of Education, 14, 3, 333-345

APTER, S. J. (1982). Troubled Children, Troubled Systems. New York: Pergamon Press

ARMSTRONG, D., GALLOWAY, D. & TOMLINSON, S. (1993). "Assessing special educational needs: the child's contribution." British Educational Research Journal, 19, 2, 121-131

ARNOLD, F. (1994). "Bullying, a tale of everyday life: reflections on insider research." Educational Action Research, 2, 2, 183-193

ARORA, C.M.J. (1994). "Is there any point in trying to reduce bullying in secondary schools? A two year follow-up of a whole school anti-bullying policy in one school." Educational Psychology in Practice, 10, 3, 155-162

ASHFORD, P. (1994). "Who is excluded from School? Does family status have an influence?" Pastoral Care in Education, 12, 4, 10-11

BARRETT, G. (1984). Getting It In Your Brain. In SCHOSTAK, J.F. & LOGAN, T. (Eds) Pupil Experience. London: Croom Helm

BARROW, G. (1995). " Behaviour support: moving towards an eco-systemic model." Therapeutic Care and Education, 4, 2, 48-53

BECKER, H. S. (1963). Outsiders: Studies in the Sociology of Deviance. New York: Free Press

BESAG, V. (1989). Bullies and Victims in Schools. Buckingham: Open University Press

BIRD, C., CHESSUM, R., FURLONG, J. & JOHNSON, D. (1981). Disaffected Pupils. Uxbridge: Brunel University

BLISHEN, E. (1969). The School That I'd Like. Harmonsworth: Penguin

BLYTH, E. & MILNER, J. (1994). "Exclusion from school and victim-blaming." Oxford Review of Education, 20, 3, 293-306

BOULTON, M. J. (1993a). "A comparison of adults' and childrens' abilities to distinguish between aggressive and playful fighting in middle school pupils: implications for playground supervision and behaviour management." Educational Studies, 19, 2, 193-203

BOULTON, M. J. (1993b). "Proximate causes of aggressive fighting in middle school children." British Journal of Educational Psychology, 63, 2, 231-244

BOULTON, M. J. (1997). "Teachers' views on bullying: definitions, attitudes and ability to cope." British Journal of Educational Psychology, 67, 2, 223-233

BRANWHITE, T. (1994). "Bullying and student distress: beneath the tip of the iceberg." Educational Psychology, 14, 1, 59-71

CHARLTON, T. & DAVID, K. (Eds) (1989). Managing Misbehaviour. Basingstoke: MacMillan Education

CHARLTON, T. & DAVID, K. (Eds). (1993). Managing Misbehaviour in Schools. London: Routledge

CHILDREN'S ACT (1989). Guidance and Regulations. London: HMSO

CLARIZIO, H. (1992). "Social maladjustment and emotional disturbance." Psychology in the Schools, 29, 2, 131-140

COLEMAN REPORT (1966). Equality of Educational Opportunity. Washington: US Government Printing Office

CONNOR, M. J. (1994). "Emotional and behavioural disorders: classification and provision." Therapeutic Care and Education, 3, 1, 4-18

COOPER, P. (1989). Respite, relationships and resignification: a study of the effects of residential schooling on pupils with emotional and behavioural difficulties, with particular reference to the pupils' perspective. Unpublished Ph.D. thesis. University of Birmingham.

COOPER, P. (1992). "Exploring pupils' perceptions of the effects of residential schooling on children with emotional and behavioural difficulties." Therapeutic Care and Education, 1, 1, 22-34

COOPER, P. (1993a). "Learning from pupils' perspectives." British Journal of Special Education, 20, 4, 129-132

COOPER, P. (1993b). "Improving the behaviour and academic performance of pupils through the curriculum." Therapeutic Care and Education, 2, 1, 252-260

COOPER, P. (1994). "Attention deficit hyperactivity disorder and the strange case of Vincent Van Gogh." Therapeutic Care and Education, 3, 2, 86-95

COOPER, P. (1996). "Giving it a name: the value of descriptive categories in educational approaches to emotional and behavioural difficulties." Support for Learning, 11, 4, 146-150

COOPER, P. (1999). "Changing perceptions of emotional and behavioural difficulties: maladjustment , EBD and beyond." Emotional and Behavioural Difficulties, 4, 1, 3-11

COOPER, P., SMITH, C. J. & UPTON, G. (1994). Emotional and Behavioural Difficulties: Theory to Practice. London: Routledge

CORBETT, J. & NORWICH, B. (1997). "Special needs and client rights: the changing social and political context of special educational research." British Educational Research Journal, 23, 3, 379-389

CRONK, K. (1987). Teacher Pupil Conflict in Secondary Schools. London: Falmer Press

CULLINGFORD, C. (1991). The Inner World of the School: Children's Ideas about School. London: Cassell

CULLINGFORD, C. (1993a). "Children's attitudes to bullying." Education 3-13, 21, 2, 54-60

CULLINGFORD, C. (1993b). "Childrens' views on gender issues in school." British Educational Research Journal, 19, 5, 555-563

RANDALL, P. (1996). A Community Approach to Bullying. Stoke: Trentham

REID, K. (1985). Truancy and School Absenteeism. London: Hodder and Stoughton

REID, K. (1986). Disaffection From School. London: Methuen

REID, K., HOPKINS, D. & HOLLY, P. (1987). Towards the Effective School. Oxford: Basil Blackwell

REYNOLDS, D. & CUTTANCE, P. (1992). School Effectiveness Research. London: Cassell

ROBINSON, G. & MAINES, B. (1997). Crying for Help: the No Blame Approach to Bullying. Bristol: Lucky Duck Publishing

RUDDOCK, J., CHAPLAIN, R. & WALLACE, G. (1995). What Can Pupils Tell Us? London: David Fulton

RUTTER, M., MAUGHAN, B., MORTIMORE, P. & OUSTON, J. (1979). Fifteen Thousand Hours. London: Open Books

SCHERER, M., GERSCH, I. & FRY, L. (Eds). (1990). Meeting Disruptive Behaviour: Assessments, Interventions and Partnership. Basingstoke: Mac-Millan

SCHOSTAK, J.F. (1983). Maladjusted Schooling. London: Falmer Press

SHARP, S. (1995). "How much does bullying hurt? The effects of bullying on the personal well-being and educational progress of secondary aged students." Educational and Child Psychology, 12, 2, 81-88

SIANN, G., CALLAGHAN, M., LOCKHART, R. & RAWSON, L. (1993). "Bullying: teachers' views and school effects." Educational Studies, 19, 3, 307-321

SIANN, G., CALLAGHAN, M. GLISSOV, P., LOCKHART, R. & RAWSON, L. (1994). "Who gets bullied? The effect of school, gender and ethnic group." Educational Research, 36, 2, 123-134

SLEE, R. (1994). "Finding a student voice in school reform: student disaffection, pathologies of disruption and educational control." International Studies in the Sociology of Education, 4, 2, 147-172

STEVENSON, R.B. & ELLSWORTH, J. (1991). "Dropping out in a working class high school: adolescent voices on the decision to leave." British Journal of Sociology of Education, 12, 3, 277-291

TATTUM, D. (1982). Disruptive Pupils in Schools and Units. Chichester: Wiley and Sons

TATTUM, D. (1984). Disruptive Pupils: Systems Rejects. In SCHOSTAK, J. F. & LOGAN, T. (Eds). Pupil Experience. London: Croom Helm

TIMES EDUCATIONAL SUPPLEMENT (TES) (1992). "Shout and be damned." 29/5/92 p10

TIMES EDUCATIONAL SUPPLEMENT (TES) (1995). "Classes are already overcrowded." 28/4/94 p13

TIMES EDUCATIONAL SUPPLEMENT (TES) (1996a). "Rise in primary exclusions." 1/11/96 p1

TIMES EDUCATIONAL SUPPLEMENT (TES) (1996b). "Exclusions rise relentlessly." 8/11/96 p1

TISDALL, G, & DAWSON, R. (1994). "Listening to the children: interviews with children attending a mainstream support facility." Support for Learning, 9, 4, 179-182

TROYNA, B. (1994). "Blind faith? Empowerment and educational research." International Studies in Sociology of Education, 4, 1, 3-24

UPTON, G. (1983). Educating Children with Behaviour Problems. Cardiff: University College

UPTON, G. & COOPER, P. (1990). "A new perspective on behaviour problems in schools: the ecosytemic approach." Maladjustment and Therapeutic Education, 8, 1, 3-18

VIVIAN, L. (1994). "The changing pupil-population of schools for pupils with emotional and behavioural difficulties." Therapeutic Care and Education, 3, 3, 218-231

WADE, B. & MOORE, M. (1993). Experiencing Special Education. Milton Keynes: Open University Press

WEDGE, P. & ESSEN, J. (1982). Children in Adversity. London: Pan

WHITNEY, I., NABUZOKA, D. & SMITH, P.K. (1992). "Bullying in schools: mainstream and special needs." Support for Learning, 7, 1, 3-7

WILLS, W.D. (1941). The Hawkspur Experiment. London: Allen and Unwin

WILLS, W.D. (1945). The Barns Experiment. London: Allen and Unwin

WILLIS, P. (1977). Learning to Labour. Farnborough: Saxon House

WISE, S. F., (1997) The behaviour of pupils with EBD and their perceptions of the factors and processes that are significant in relation to their own behaviour and resulting placement in special education. Unpublished Ph.D. thesis. University of Birmingham.

WOLFF, L. (1993). "Does behaviour really matter?" Therapeutic Care and Education, 2, 1, 216-221

WOODS, P. (1977). The Ethnography of the School. Block 11, Units 7-8. Milton Keynes: Open University Press

WOODS, P. (Ed). (1980). Pupil Strategies. London: Croom Helm

WOODS, P. (1983). Sociology and the School: An Interactionist Viewpoint. London: Routledge and Kegan Paul

WOODS, P. (1990). Happiest Days: How Pupils Cope With School. Lewes: Falmer Press

YOUNG, S. (1998). The support group approach to bullying in schools. Educational Psychology in Practice, 14,1 32-39